Dear Mark,

I'm truly grateful for the opportunity to meet with you and the Board. I'm equally excited to be your new neighbor and to become part of this beautiful community.

As you read through my book, you'll quickly see that real estate runs in my DNA. I've been incredibly blessed to inherit passion, perseverance and resilience from those brave souls who came before me, qualities that continue to guide me every day.

With appreciation and excitement for what's ahead.

Josephine

Mama Nonne

PALMETTO
PUBLISHING
Charleston, SC
www.PalmettoPublishing.com

Charleston, SC
www.PalmettoPublishing.com

Mama Nonne
Copyright © 2023 by Josephine Traina, LLC
www.josephinetraina.com

All rights reserved
No portion of this book may be reproduced, stored in a retrieval system, or transmitted in any form by any means—electronic, mechanical, photocopy, recording, or other—except for brief quotations in printed reviews, without prior permission of the author.

First Edition

Hardcover ISBN: 979-8-8229-1587-9
Paperback ISBN: 979-8-8229-1588-6

Mama Nonne

A SICILIAN IMMIGRANT TALE OF SACRIFICE, LACK AND CONTROL

JOSEPHINE TRAINA

Vita, Trapani Sicily

Per la mia famiglia,

My son, Thomas, my daughter, Alexis, grandchildren, Hannah, Chase, Evelina, Sebastian, Julian, and my Bonus son, Amit, and Bonus daughter, Heather.

Ti amo,
Mom

Contents

Dedication xi

Preface xiii

Acknowledgments xvii

About the Author xix

Pietronilla Angeleri & Baldassare Rizzuto 1

The Crossing to Ellis Island 5

Ellis Island 8

Life In America 12

Josephine Rizzuto & Nicola Sciacca 16

The Family Home on Suydam Street 20

Motherless Daughters 24

Your Mother Is Always With You 27

The Belle Sorelle: The Beautiful Sisters 28

Crucifissa Sciacca Dolzani 29

Pietronilla Sciacca Impellizzeri 32

Maria Anna Sciacca Traina 36

Mama Nonne 42

Epilogue 47

Souls of the Dearly Departed 51

Family Tree 53

La Cucina: Cooking is a Gesture of Love 55

Family Recipes 56

Blossoming With Grace at Every Age 103

Bibliography 105

History & Family Discoveries 111

"He who has a why to live for, can bear with almost any how."
—**Friedrich Nietzsche**

Dedication

This book is a tribute to my great-grandmother, Mama Nonne, spiritual caretaker and matriarch, the backbone of the family, and the one who kept a roof over the family's heads during the darkest of times. She was truly the only constant in the young lives of my mother and her two sisters. Her "why" was her hunger to follow her dream of a better life for the unborn child she carried on the transatlantic journey to America. That child would become my grandmother and namesake, Josephine.

The book's title refers to the old Sicilian and southern Italian ways and belief systems of sacrifice, lack, and control, which crossed the Atlantic Ocean with Mama Nonne. The immigrant mindset was full of scarcity and burdens, and for women, being controlled by fathers, husbands, and the Catholic Church. Mama Nonne's courage in the face of these challenges makes her the heroine of the story, the one who gave her life to something larger than herself.

I am so fortunate to have an incredible role model like Mama Nonne. She was a shining example of love and integrity. Her strength lives on in me and our entire family. I am in awe of what the immigrants in my family experienced and how they survived. I'm both proud and humbled to be the great-granddaughter of this beautiful soul we called Mama Nonne.

"Roots are not in landscape or a country, or a people, they are inside you."

—Isabel Allende

Preface

I am descended from one of the many Sicilian and Italian families who immigrated to America seeking a better life. I have always been curious about where they came from, and how they survived and eventually thrived in America. These brave relatives sacrificed so their children would have a better life than theirs. They left behind everyone they knew in Sicily to start life in a strange new country with unfamiliar languages and customs. My maternal great-grandparents eventually achieved the American dream of homeownership, something they might never have believed possible.

Over twenty years ago, I set out to create a cookbook of favorite family recipes and memories to honor my mother and her two sisters. They had all passed away, and I was eager to capture loving memories for the families they left behind. After starting and stopping several times, I found myself going in a completely different direction. Many hours of research later, the project eventually became much more than a collection of recipes and memories. I delved into historical documents and managed to piece together some of the story of how relatives on my mother's side of the family traveled to and settled in America. This book recounts who they were, why and how they came to America, how they lived once they got here, and what kind of legacy they left behind for us. Most of the family members I write about are long gone, leaving us with only their memories to keep them alive in our hearts. I discovered I have many more relatives than I ever knew about. I did not have time to research them all, but I hope this book makes its way into their hands.

My great-grandparents hoped to get to America, the land of opportunity, so they and future generations could break the patterns of poverty and suffering. Making the journey to America with little more than the clothes on their backs, I can only imagine how they must have felt on their eighteen-day voyage across the Atlantic Ocean. They had probably never traveled far from the small town where they were born. They displayed perseverance and resilience and abiding hope they would build a new life for themselves. They would eventually have children and create a family who would not only survive but would thrive in their new country.

The sources of this tale include online and print genealogical research, as well as recollections of family members. It was a journey of self-discovery, as I imagined myself walking in the shoes of my great-grandparents and their children and making connections to my own life. I hope the stories paint a picture of what the previous generations experienced amid their laughter and tears. I hope future generations will feel the souls of those they never met. I have tried to give voice to those who came before us, to bring them out of the shadows and into the light, so their stories and courageous actions and sacrifices will not be forgotten.

This book is my gift to my family and all the Sicilian and Italian immigrants who made the perilous journey across the Atlantic Ocean, a 3,000-mile voyage which would change their lives. This book is written from my heart. I have come to understand I can't really know who I am unless I know about who came before me.

May this book inspire you to find your roots!

Josephine Traina
Atlanta, Georgia

Special thanks to Mas Sajady, whose work was the inspiration for the title of this book. As you will read in the following pages, these dearly departed Sicilian immigrants had to sacrifice greatly so the next generation wouldn't have to.

He helped me to understand how generational traits, good or bad, can be passed down from one generation to the next, recycling family patterns. Mas guided me to look within for happiness, not outside of myself.

And to Fei Sajady for her inspiring words used in the epilogue of this book.

Thank you, Tony Robbins, my mentor.

When I began the journey of writing about how my family became Americans, I had no idea where to start. My wise teacher, Tony Robbins' quote, "Don't get caught in the tyranny of how," was ever present in my mind as I attempted and failed many times to complete my book. Tony taught me to focus on the outcome, not the obstacles. I knew that I would succeed if I did not allow the "tyranny of how" to stop me.

All I have learned about building a business and attaining financial freedom were gifts Tony shared with this seeker. I am forever thankful for the life lessons and this quote:

"Life is always happening for us, not to us."

There are few people who leave footprints on your heart. Joseph McClendon III is one of them.

His kindness and generosity of spirit at Leadership Academy are gifts I will always cherish. Thank you, Joseph, for all the life lessons. I am forever grateful.

Acknowledgments & Special Thanks

A special thanks to my sister, Stefani. Her editing and organizational skills are epic. Her keen insight and ongoing support in bringing my stories to life have been a true blessing. Because of her efforts and encouragement, I have a legacy to pass on to my family where one did not exist before.

A special thanks to Andy Hampton, who discovered essential information about my family's journey to America. He also edited the photographs on the cover and throughout the book. I am forever grateful for his assistance with this project.

More special thanks to my sisters and cousins for sharing their photographs and memories of the dear women in our family.

"There is no greater agony than bearing an untold story inside you."

—Maya Angelou

About the Author

My maternal great-grandparents invested in real estate during the 1920s and 1930s, extremely turbulent times. Over time, they owned four different properties in the Bushwick section of Brooklyn, New York. I like to believe I inherited my drive, determination, perseverance, and resilience from these two brave souls. I believe they passed on to me their love of real estate and their entrepreneurial spirit. I began my real estate career knocking on strangers' doors (cold calling) and experiencing many rejections, probably not all that different from my great-grandparents who were navigating their new land as immigrants.

In 1978, I was living in a shabby apartment with my four-year-old son. I was determined to move us to a better situation. One cold, January day, I knocked on a door and a pregnant woman answered. As fate would have it, she was looking to sell her house. I could not believe my good fortune. Standing on one side of that door was a mother-to-be who wanted to sell her house, and on the other side was me, a divorced, single mother looking to buy one. The only obstacle was I did not qualify for a conventional mortgage. My family thought it was risky, but I secured a non-qualifying loan at 8% interest and bought my first property in my own name. Now I realize my great-grandparents' spirit was urging me to invest in real estate and build a safe, secure life for myself and my young son. I had no guaranteed income, but I had achieved the American dream of homeownership against all odds, like them. I made choices and sacrifices so my son would have a better life…that's all I knew how to do. That house would eventually become a rental property. Later in my career, I would be chosen by the National Association of REALTORS® to appear in a public service advertising campaign about how realtors help people achieve the American dream of homeownership.

I bought my first piece of real estate when I was twenty-three years old and married, and my second when I was thirty and divorced. Other properties have come and gone over the years. I once juggled owning four at the same time. Fast forward to May 2002, a short time after the 9/11 tragedy. I spearheaded the Atlanta Board of REALTORS® Italian Festival fundraiser, La Dolce Vita. The funds we raised helped build the first Habitat for Humanity home in Atlanta. A single mother and her young son were chosen to be the new homeowners. When I look back on this project and how meaningful it was for me, I realize it connected me with those early years in my own life. I felt so privileged to pay it forward so another mother could have the American dream of homeownership and raise her son in a safe, secure environment.

After owning my own real estate firm and working as a real estate broker for several companies in Atlanta, I followed my daughter to Charleston, South Carolina, where my entrepreneurial spirit continued. I became the broker and marketing director for Bee Street Lofts, a new 108-unit condominium building across from the Medical University of South Carolina. After the financial downturn in 2008, the real estate market in Charleston was in a serious downturn. The building had lost its financing, which made it challenging to sell units. I invested $10,000 of my own money and created a successful marketing campaign geared to medical professionals. I set up the special doctor loan program, secured financing for the building, and eventually sold out all the units. I also established the "My Heavenly Reward" program, whereby I donated a portion of every real estate commission in my clients' names to support their favorite charity. Through that program, I was able to donate over $30,000 to support Roper St. Francis Hospital, Medical University of South Carolina Hospital, MUSC Hollings Cancer Center, the Ronald McDonald Charities, and MUSC Children's Hospitals. I also supported Doctors Without Borders, and the Charleston Animal Society's yearly fundraiser.

With over forty years of real estate and entrepreneurial experience behind me, I've now turned my attention to coaching and mentoring. My mission for the rest of my life is to share all the life lessons I have learned as an entrepreneur so that I may assist others on their path to success.

Author and her son
and their new home, 1978

Auction flyer for Habitat
for Humanity, 2002

Atlanta REALTOR, The Board
Builds A House, 2003

Top Agent Magazine cover, May 2013

Author and new owners of
Habit for Humanity home, 2003

"Throughout the history of the human race no land and no people have suffered so terribly from slavery, from foreign conquests and oppressions, and none has struggled so irrepressibly for emancipation as Sicily and the Sicilians. Almost from the time when Polyphemus promenaded around Etna, or when Ceres taught the Siculi the culture of grain, to our day, Sicily has been the theater of uninterrupted invasions and wars, and of unflinching resistance. The Sicilians are a mixture of almost all southern and northern races; first, of the aboriginal Sicanians, with Phoenicians, Carthaginians, Greeks, and slaves from all regions under heaven, imported into the island by traffic or war; and then of Arabs, Normans, and Italians. The Sicilians, in all these transformations and modifications, have battled, and still battle, for their freedom."

–Karl Marx, New-York Tribune, May 17, 1860

Pietronilla Angeleri & Baldassare Rizzuto

The story begins in Vita, Sicily, a tiny town of 3.3 square miles, a little over 50 miles southwest of Palermo, in the province of Trapani. My maternal great-grandfather, Baldassare Rizzuto, was born there in 1865 or 1869 (records vary), the son of Pietro and Giuseppa Monica (Modica) Rizzuto. He had four siblings, Melchiore, Antonina, Nicolo and Giuseppe. My maternal great-grandmother, Pietronilla Angeleri (Mama Nonne), was born on April 23, 1870, to Baldassare and Leonarda (Renda) Angeleri. She had three sisters, Maria, Angela, and Giuseppina (Josephine).

On October 4, 1899, Mama Nonne married Baldassare Rizzuto. Six months later, these two brave souls and six other family members boarded the *SS Sempione* and departed from the port of Palermo, two days shy of Mama Nonne's thirtieth birthday. These Sicilian immigrants, who could not read or write English, left everything behind except for the clothes on their backs and a few bags. What could have been going through their minds as they set out on their journey to a better life? Were they terrified the boat would sink? Did they wonder whether they would be allowed to stay in America once they arrived? They sacrificed everything they had to make a better life for themselves and their family. There was no turning back.

Josephine Traina

Why They Left Sicily

The Kingdom of Italy was officially created in 1861, when several separate states formerly allied with other European countries, voted to become a new unified country under King Victor Emmanuel II. The Italian kingdom grew to its final size after incorporating Venetia and Rome in 1871. Although Sicily had been in favor of unification, the process and its aftermath were not without severe economic and social consequences. Decades of political turmoil had contributed to the profound economic disparities between the north and south. When the new government imposed higher taxes and mandatory military service, the poorer citizens in the mostly rural south found themselves in an increasingly difficult situation. The cycle of poverty was made worse by outbreaks of contagious diseases and unrelenting erosion of farmland. Farmers couldn't grow enough to feed themselves. The government's promises to provide land kept many peasants trapped when they couldn't pay off their loans.

By the late nineteenth century, life in southern Italy and Sicily had become nearly intolerable. As the cost of travel became more affordable, and word spread about better opportunities in America, Sicilians and southern Italians made plans to leave their homeland. My great-grandparents, like so many others, had limited options for improving their lives in Sicily. They could not survive in their own country, so they had to escape, and escape they did. They left behind poverty, high mortality rates, malnutrition and semi-starvation, crime, unemployment, underemployment, poor medical care, inadequate schooling, poor housing, a rigid class structure and exploitation. For the average Sicilian peasant living in these dismal conditions, immigrating to America was an opportunity for liberation and a better life. After all, wasn't the United States supposed to be the land of opportunity?

Sicilian & Italian Women: Sacrifice, Lack, and Control

Many poor women in Sicily and southern Italy in the late nineteenth and early twentieth century were subjected to lives filled with sacrifice, lack (burdens), and control, which came in the form of governmental control, control by husbands and fathers, and control by the Catholic Church. In a nutshell, these women were often resigned to the fact that "life brutalizes." They were treated as second-class citizens. Many wore rags and did without so their children could be dressed properly. A woman could not apply for a passport without her husband's written consent.

The life circumstances of these women who lived in deep poverty, contributed to their limited world view and their pessimism that anything would change or improve. The profound lack of resources left them almost no way to escape the old feuds and lack of learning opportunities. There was a strong tendency to indulge sons over daughters, which continued the pattern of women being subservient to men. For many of these women, even though they often managed the family finances, being able to sign one's name was good enough. A very common mindset was one of pessimism and mistrust of others, including the government, which failed to provide desperately needed help. This was the environment and time when Mama Nonne was born in 1870 in Vita, Sicily. Who wouldn't have wanted to escape this barely survivable existence?

Sicilian woman carrying water

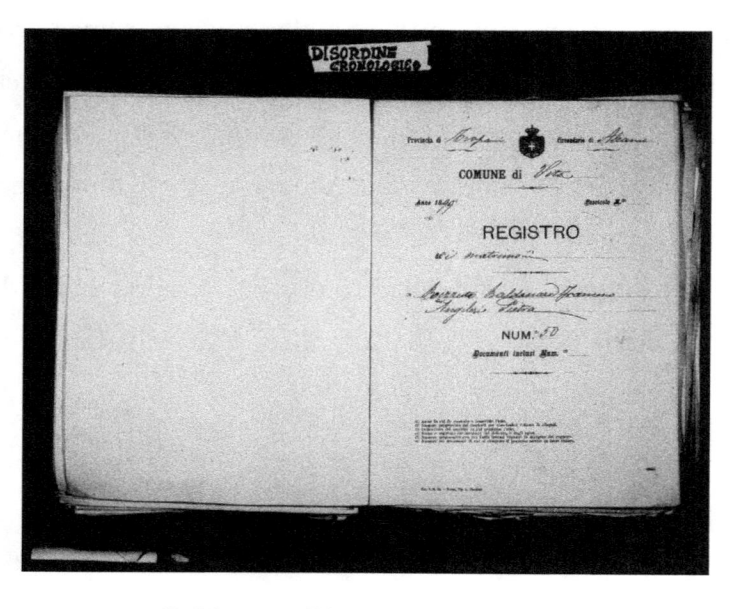

Baldassare Rizzuto & Pietronilla
Angeleri Marriage Registry, 1899

Sicilian women in the countryside

Sicilian girl carrying water

"Out of suffering have emerged the strongest souls; the most massive characters are seared with scars."

–Khalil Gibran

The Crossing to Ellis Island

Immigrating to the United States required enormous sacrifices. Immigrants longed for a better life, but they faced serious risks, both on the journey and after they arrived. Many Sicilians and Italians decided to leave the only home they knew for an unknown country, America, with the hope that they would be free to make their own decisions instead of being controlled by the government in the old country. When I think of Mama Nonne and Baldassare, I imagine that sadness must have washed over them as they resigned themselves to leaving Sicily without knowing what the outcome might be.

The *SS Sempione*

Pietro (Peter) LaGrassa was the first family member to come to America in 1898. He was married to Mama Nonne's sister, Josephine, and they had three children, all born in Sicily. Peter got a job and found a place to live, and he most likely sent his wife and her family the money for their steerage tickets on the *SS Sempione*. It was common practice at that time for relatives in America to pay for the tickets of those immigrating from Sicily and Italy. The average price for a ticket in the steerage compartment of a steamship was about $30 per person in those days. Steamship companies employed ticket salesmen who traveled around Europe, selling tickets to travelers. Transporting immigrants was a lucrative business. Peter was listed as the sponsor on the family's immigration documents, and he set up housing for them when they arrived.

After obtaining their tickets, my great-grandparents would have obtained passports from the Italian authorities and arranged to travel the fifty miles from Vita to Palermo to meet their ship. They would have coordinated their departure according to the date on their tickets, and this must have been a challenge for

Josephine Traina

people who had probably never traveled much beyond their small village. They would have traveled to Palermo by train, wagon, donkey, or even on foot. Once they finally arrived at the port, if their paperwork and documents were in order, they would have found some kind of lodging until the day came when they could board the ship and depart for America.

The United States Immigration Act of 1893 required ship manifests to be submitted to an Immigration Inspector at the port from which the ship departed. The inspector had the power to deny passage to anyone who didn't meet specific criteria. Detailed information was collected for each passenger: their full name, age, sex, marital status, nationality, occupation, height, mental and physical health, last residence, port destination, final destination, if they were joining a relative, and their name and address, if they could read or write and in what language, who paid for their ticket, if they had ever been deported from America, if they'd ever been in prison, if they were a polygamist or an anarchist, if they had work lined up, and if they had any money. Before they were allowed to board the ship, passengers were examined for signs of infectious diseases by a doctor working for the steamship company. Finally, they and their belongings were sprayed with disinfectant.

My great-grandparents boarded the *SS Sempione* with all their worldly possessions and departed from Palermo, Sicily on April 21, 1900. Their entourage of eight people included Mama Nonne's three sisters, Josephine LaGrassa, Angela Angeleri, and Maria Angeleri, and Josephine's three children, Salvatore, Christina and Baldassare. My great-grandfather was the only man accompanying this group of women and children. His own wife was pregnant. He must have felt a huge sense of responsibility for these vulnerable travelers.

Since tickets in the steerage compartment were sold without designated passenger space, travelers were crammed by the hundreds into one of the lowest levels of the ship. The *SS Sempione* transported 1,500 passengers, with 1,100 housed in steerage. Steerage passengers endured limited or no access to bathrooms, and very poor ventilation during storms when deck hatches were closed. They were often confined to spending most of their time below deck, seasick, cooking and sleeping and sharing space with hundreds of others. Beds were single and double bunks meant to be shared. With so many people occupying the same space, diseases spread quickly, and buckets which served as toilets contributed to the overall unsanitary conditions.

I wonder what expectations my relatives had before they boarded the ship, and if they were dismayed when they saw where they would be confined for the next eighteen days. Mama Nonne was four months pregnant during this journey, and she no doubt struggled with the conditions. I can only imagine how she and her family endured and survived this harrowing ordeal. They had likely decided there was no turning back, and they had no choice but to persevere and to try to stay healthy. I like to believe Mama Nonne was very wise, as she must have known the child she carried would be the first in the family to become an American citizen by birth. Her daughter, my grandmother, Josephine, would be born five months later on October 9, 1900, in their new home in Brooklyn, New York.

> "Give me your tired, your poor,
> Your huddled masses yearning to breathe free,
> The wretched refuse of your teeming shore.
> Send these, the homeless, tempest-tost to me,
> I lift my lamp beside the golden door!"
>
> –from The New Colossus by Emma Lazarus

Ellis Island

After crossing the Atlantic Ocean and entering New York Harbor, the next step on their journey was to make it through the inspections at Ellis Island, which was just past the Statue of Liberty, half a mile to the northwest. The *SS Sempione* landed at Ellis Island on May 11, 1900.

First and second-class passengers arriving in New York Harbor were not required to undergo the inspection process at Ellis Island. Instead, they received a cursory inspection aboard the ship, the theory being if a person could afford to purchase a first or second-class ticket, they were affluent and less likely to become a public charge in America for medical or legal reasons. Any sick passengers and those with legal problems were sent on to Ellis Island for further inspection.

The scenario was far different for third class or steerage passengers. After the steamship docked, these passengers would board a barge to Ellis Island. Each passenger was required to wear a nametag with their manifest number in big letters. They were organized by number and loaded onto the barges, along with their belongings, which were stowed below deck.

Once they arrived at Ellis Island and disembarked from the barge, the next challenge for Mama Nonne and her family was the battery of mental and physical examinations. How confusing and stressful it must have been to be in a crowd with so many people, especially after being confined in the lower compartment of a ship for almost three weeks. They would have been asked to line up for their medical examinations. They may have still been wobbling and seasick from their long voyage. Their ears would have been assaulted by a barrage of unfamiliar languages being spoken. While they lined up, they would have encountered their first American, an interpreter. These translators were eventually called unsung heroes for their persistence and expertise, which frequently helped immigrants avoid being deported. An interpreter often spoke several languages, and it was not unusual for some to speak a dozen languages, including dialects.

The interpreters guided groups of people through the main entrance and up a flight of stairs to the Registry Room (Great Hall). As they were climbing the stairs, a surgeon with the U.S. Public Health Service observed the immigrants, looking for signs of contagious diseases like trachoma, tuberculosis, and diphtheria, as well as any signs of lameness, heart difficulties, breathing difficulties, or mental disabilities. As they passed, the surgeon would check the face, hair, neck and hands of each traveler, and mark with chalk and remove from the line anyone who required additional physical or mental examinations or treatment. Occasionally, groups were required to bathe in disinfectant. Pregnancy was noted in chalk with the letters PG. My great-grandmother, four months pregnant, may have had PG written on her. The painful eye examinations for trachoma, a condition which could cause death or blindness, were the source of more than half of the medical detentions. Being diagnosed with trachoma meant you would almost certainly be deported. The inspections took place in the Great Hall, where doctors would briefly scan every individual for obvious physical ailments.

The next step was the legal inspection. The ship's manifest log, initially filled out at the ship's port of departure, contained each immigrant's name and answers to 29 questions. This document was used by the legal inspectors to cross-examine immigrants. Contrary to popular belief, interpreters of all major languages were employed at Ellis Island, making the process efficient and ensuring that records were accurate.

Despite the island's reputation as an "Island of Tears," most immigrants were treated courteously and respectfully, free to begin their new lives in America after only a few short hours on Ellis Island. If an immigrant's papers were in order and they were in reasonably good health, the inspection process lasted 3 to 5 hours. Only two percent of the arriving immigrants were excluded from entry. The two main reasons for exclusion were a doctor diagnosing an immigrant with a contagious disease that could endanger the public health, or a legal inspector was concerned an immigrant would likely become a public charge or an illegal contract laborer.

Their journey to and through Ellis Island complete, immigrants would obtain their boxed lunches and automobile, train, or ferry permits. The ferry terminal had designated spaces for each independent train line where immigrants could wait. Many had started their journey months or even years before, yet no matter what lay ahead, they could read the sign that said, "Welcome to America."

Josephine Traina

My great-grandfather arrived in America with eighteen dollars in his pocket and a burning desire to make a better life for his family. I can only begin to imagine how deeply exhausting this experience was for everyone. Sicilian and Italian immigrants came mainly from the Trapani region of Sicily, where Mama Nonne and Baldassare were born, and Apulia and Calabria in southern Italy. Nearly eighty percent of them entered the country through Ellis Island. I am in awe of their strength and what they endured for the promise of a better life.

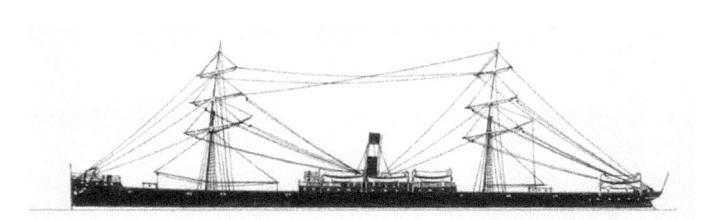

The *SS Sempione*

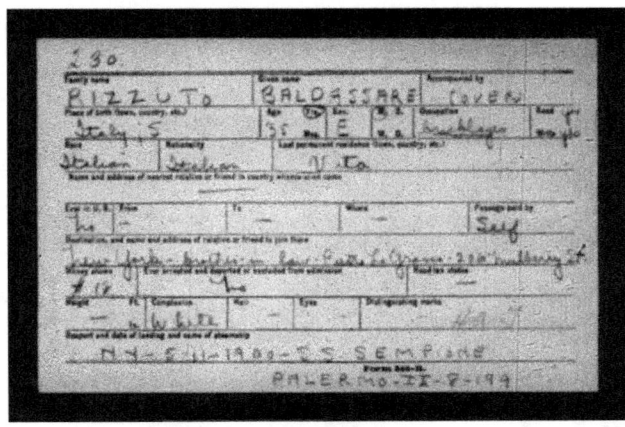

My great-grandfather's *SS Sempione* card

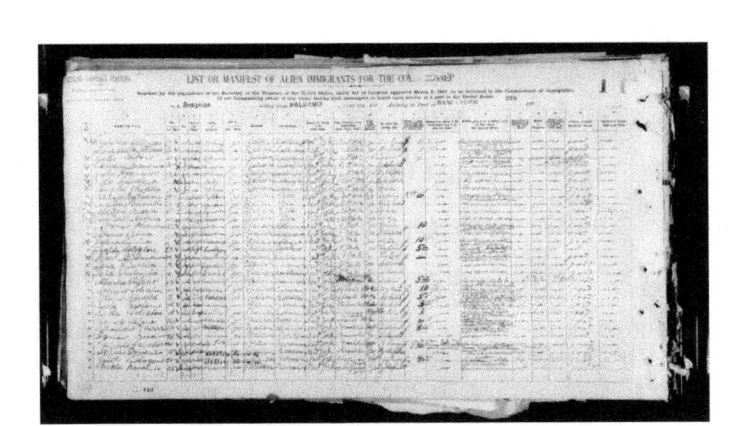

My relatives listed on the
SS Sempione manifest

Immigrants approaching the
Statue of Liberty, *Getty Images*

The Great Hall, Ellis Island,
Getty Images

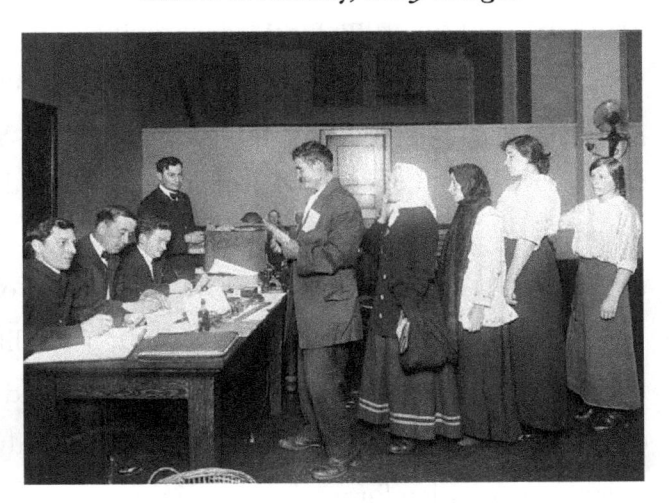

New arrivals being processed at
Ellis Island, *Getty Images*

> "Even in our sleep, pain which cannot forget, falls drop by drop upon the heart, until in our own despair, against our will, comes wisdom, through the awful grace of God."
>
> -Aeschylus c.525-456 BC

Life In America

My quest to learn about my maternal ancestors was fueled by the discovery of passenger records and census records for Mama Nonne and Baldassare. They were a treasure trove of information and helped paint a picture of their lives. Misspelling of their names aside, birth, marriage, census and death records were invaluable. This is a partial story of some of the relatives who came over together on the *SS Sempione* to make lives in America. I did not know about Mama Nonne's three sisters, or that her brother-in-law, Peter La Grassa, came over to set things up so the rest of the family could join him. I extend a grateful nod to him for working so hard and making it possible for our family to travel to America.

The Sicilian and southern Italian belief systems, which crossed the Atlantic Ocean with Mama Nonne and the others, dictated their lives in America. Their worldview was filled with sacrifice, scarcity, lack (burdens), and for women especially, control by fathers, husbands, and the Catholic Church. Children were expected to be baptized and receive the sacraments. There were strong patriarchal pressures to preserve the family honor and marry off daughters at an early age. The only way a Sicilian or Italian girl could leave her family was by getting married. Fathers also had a lot of control over sons, expecting them to follow in their footsteps or abide by their rules. Many Sicilian and Italian immigrants went along with the rules of the church because it was their place of solace in a cruel world.

With little education and no hope for a better life, many Sicilian and Italian immigrants were forced to find work in sweatshops. They were the lowest paid workers in America during Mama Nonne's time in the early twentieth century. Poor immigrants frequently worked fifteen to eighteen hours a day because of the intense competition for work and their urgent need for the job. Much of the labor for the industrial expansion in the United States came from waves of Italian and Sicilian immigrants, and this was the competitive work environment my great-grandparents faced when they arrived in America. Their willingness to work for lower wages than others made them very unpopular, which is why they congregated in Sicilian and Italian enclaves to protect themselves from a hostile outside world.

Mama Nonne and Baldassare settled in the Bushwick section of Brooklyn, New York. Bushwick was becoming an Italian enclave, and they would have become familiar with the shops and shopkeepers. Since they spoke the same language, they didn't have to learn English, although both of them would eventually learn to read and write. They may have felt safe and protected in their own community with mostly Sicilian and Italian neighbors looking out for each other.

Upon arrival in America in 1900, Mama Nonne and her family lived together on Boerum Street in Bushwick. The women worked in sweatshops, like so many immigrants. Baldassare worked as a bricklayer and Peter LaGrassa as a piano maker. Nine family members were crowded into one apartment: Mamma Nonne, Baldassare, Peter, Josephine, their three children, and Mama Nonne's two sisters, Angela, and Maria. In October of 1900, Mama Nonne's daughter, Josephine, my grandmother, was born. She was the first American citizen in the family.

Two years later, Mama Nonne gave birth to a son, Pietro, but sadly, he died of pneumonia at fifteen months of age. Walking in Mama Nonne's shoes, I feel sure she wanted to move from the place which had seen the death of her first son. The entire family moved to George Street, and the next family loss was Mama Nonne's sister, Angela. Sadly, she died of tuberculosis in 1908. She was forty-seven years old.

In 1910, Baldassare was working as a laborer and Mama Nonne was at home. They were still living at George Street as renters. The census listed Baldassare as out of work for twenty weeks in 1909, which must have been a huge financial challenge. Only Josephine, who was nine years old and in school, could speak and read and write English. Mama Nonne had given birth to another son, whom they named Pietro, on June 12, 1910. She was forty years old. This was most likely Mama Nonne's final pregnancy. We were always told she had five children, but we have no details for two of them.

Between 1915 and 1920, Baldassare and Mama Nonne became real estate investors, and learned to read and write English. They bought the building on George Street, where they had previously rented. It remains a mystery how they managed to secure a mortgage and purchase a property during the turbulent markets of the early 1900s. Baldassare worked as a presser, and Mama Nonne was at home. The photograph of the Rizzuto family on the book's front cover, taken around this time, says so much. Mama Nonne has a hint of a smile as she stands between Baldassare and Pietro. Josephine lovingly drapes her arm over her father's shoulder. These Sicilian immigrants achieved the American dream of homeownership and

Josephine Traina

eventually held investments in four brownstones in Bushwick. My great-grandfather looks happy and proud, for he had much to be thankful for, a new life, a home in a new country and a beautiful family. This happiness would be short lived, as Mama Nonne's second son named Pietro would die shortly after this picture was taken.

Josephine married Nicola Sciacca in 1918, at the age of seventeen, and they lived on George Street with their daughter, Crucifissa (my Aunt Gussie). Nicola worked as a heeler in a shoe factory and Josephine was a housewife. By 1925, Baldassare and Mama Nonne had moved to 255 Jefferson Street, their third residence since coming to America. Once again, the entire family was together in the same building. Josephine and Nicola lived there with their now three children, Gussie, Beatrice and my mother, Anna. Baldassare was out of work in 1925, and this must have been a terrible hardship, especially if they were covering mortgage payments on other rental properties. Mama Nonne worked as a finisher of coats. Mama Nonne and Baldassare never became American citizens; they only had alien cards.

The next several years were filled with so much loss. Baldassare died of stomach cancer in 1927 at fifty-eight years old. Mama Nonne's sister, Josephine, died in 1928 of mitral insufficiency, probably related to rheumatic fever. She was sixty-nine years old. Her other sister, Maria Formica, died in 1932 of a cerebral hemorrhage. She was sixty-six years old. She left half of her $5,000 estate to Mama Nonne, and the other half to her two nieces, Christina Profera, Josephine LaGrassa's daughter, and Josephine Sciacca, Mama Nonne's daughter. Mama Nonne was the executor of Maria's estate.

After Baldassare's death, Mama Nonne worked in a factory by day and managed her investment properties and collected rent at night. She was left with the task of managing everything on her own. In addition to her personal losses, in late 1929, Mama Nonne witnessed the beginning of the Great Depression, a worldwide economic crisis deemed the worst of its kind in the twentieth century. The economy started to shrink months before the stock market crash in October of that year. By 1930, thirteen hundred banks had failed, and 15.5 million people were out of work. Depositors hurried to banks to withdraw their funds as bank failures increased. Of the 24,000 commercial banks in the country, only a third were part of the Federal Reserve banking system, which had stricter rules about cash reserves. The Bank of the United States failed on December 11, 1930, the largest bank failure at that time. Foreclosures escalated, and by 1933, close to half of all home mortgages were in default. There were one thousand foreclosures a day in 1933. The American economy was in dire straits.

By 1932, Mama Nonne had lost four of her children, her husband, and all three sisters who had traveled to America with her. The worst loss was yet to come, however, when her daughter, Josephine, my grandmother, died suddenly and unexpectedly on June 8, 1934, of spinal meningitis, at the age of thirty-three. She left behind her husband, Nicola, and three daughters, Gussie, age fifteen, Beatrice, age fourteen, and Anna, (my mother) age twelve. Mama Nonne would help care for her three granddaughters, who were now motherless daughters, just like she had been at the age of ten back in Sicily.

The loss of the daughter to the mother, the mother to the daughter, is the essential female tragedy."

—Adrienne Rich

Josephine Rizzuto & Nicola Sciacca

In all the photographs of my grandmother, I've always noticed a kind of sadness which emanates from her. We were always told Mama Nonne had given birth to five children. How very sad it must have been for Josephine to watch her parents bury all her siblings. When Josephine was seventeen, her parents arranged for her to marry Nicola Sciacca, another Sicilian immigrant who was nearly twelve years older. He had served in WWI as a musician in the infantry. He came from a very musical family of several brothers. They were married on June 9, 1918, and eventually had three daughters, Crucifissa (Gussie), born on February 29, 1919, Pietronella, (Beatrice) born on October 4, 1920, and my mother, Maria Anna, born on April 27, 1922. Everyone in Josephine and Nicola's family was an American citizen. Four of them had been born in America and Nicola became a naturalized citizen in 1920.

Nick Sciacca was quite dapper, impeccably dressed in white starched shirts and expensive suits. Cousin Gina told a story of how when he was walking home from work, the neighbors would run to Josephine's house to tell her to put the pot on so his pasta could be served to him as soon as he walked in the door. The women in the family, except his mother-in-law, Mama Nonne, were expected to wait on him hand and foot.

By 1930, Nick and Josephine and their three daughters were living as renters on Suydam Street, again in a building owned by Mama Nonne. Nick was working in the print shop of a family friend and Josephine worked in a dress factory. Their rent was $20 per month, the least of all the other tenants.

When I was young, my mother shared with me the tragic story of her mother's death. She came home from school one day to find her mother not feeling well. The next thing she knew, an ambulance was taking her beloved mother to the hospital, where she died the next day. Josephine Sciacca died on June 8,

1934, of spinal meningitis, at the age of thirty-three. It can be a very painful death, with inflammation of the brain causing death very quickly. Although vaccines were being developed, they were not in time to help my grandmother. Because she died of an incurable, contagious disease, the home at Suydam Street was quarantined by the health department. Their beds were burned, and a sign was posted on the door stating no one could enter or leave the house.

The guilt, shame, and sadness of this life-altering event would stay with my mother and her sisters throughout their lives. My grandmother's body was eventually brought back home for the funeral and burial. Professional wailers attended and they screamed and wailed for three days. My mother and her two sisters, now three motherless children, endured these terrible events and watched over their mother's lifeless body in the rooms where they lived and slept. Mama Nonne must have been in a state of total shock at the loss of her only daughter, her last living child. She had lost her own mother when she was ten years old, and now she was watching her three granddaughters trapped in a similar tragedy.

Ill-equipped to provide financially for his three motherless daughters, my grandfather required Gussie and Beatrice to quit school and go to work in garment factories to help support the family. They followed in the footsteps of their mother and grandmother during the Great Depression. My mother, Anna, was allowed to stay in school, but she became the family cook, learning under her father's guidance. As was the Sicilian tradition, the father expected the daughters to become the family caretakers as women had in previous generations. These adolescent daughters became involuntary mini-mothers, and their family tragedy created an indelible bond between the sisters that lasted throughout their lives.

Nick Sciacca and his three daughters lived on Suydam Street for several years after Josephine's death. Anna graduated from high school in 1940. Beatrice was the first to marry in 1941, followed by Anna and Gussie in 1943. He never owned any property, but he lived at Suydam Street by the grace of Mama Nonne. If it had not been for her, my family would have been homeless. She waited for him to come home with food and collected rent from him when she could. Generous to the end, Mama Nonne gave her property at 255 Jefferson Street, (where her beloved Baldassare had died) to Nick and his new wife, Rosalia. They lived there until he became too infirm and needed nursing care, and his wife and her family received the proceeds from the sale of the property. Nicola Sciacca died on May 16, 1977.

Despite her untimely death, Josephine Rizzuto Sciacca's legacy continued in her three beautiful daughters, their ten children, sixteen great-grandchildren and many great-great-grandchildren. We are here because of her, and although we never had the privilege to know her, her beautiful spirit lives on in each one of us. She left a legacy of love. We are that legacy of love.

Josephine, Baldassare, Mama
Nonne, Pietro Rizzuto, circa 1915

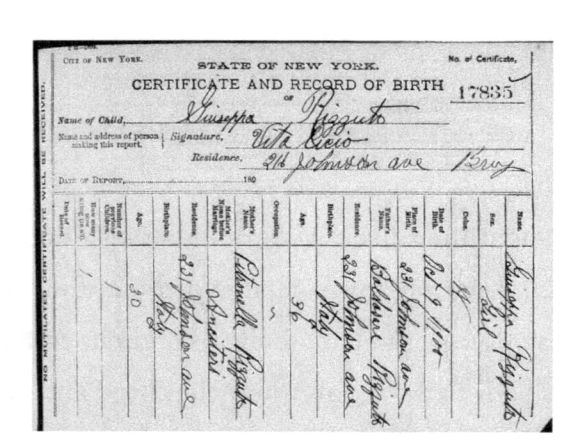

Giuseppa Rizzuto
birth certificate, October 9, 1900

Nicola Sciacca & Giuseppe
Rizzuto marriage certificate

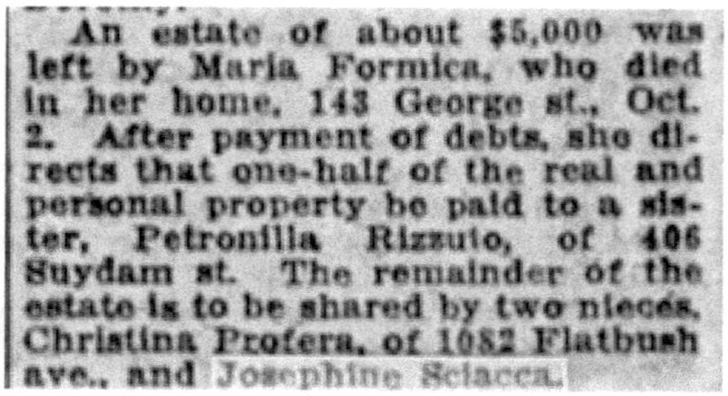

Pietronilla, Anna, Crucifissa
Sciacca, christening, circa 1924

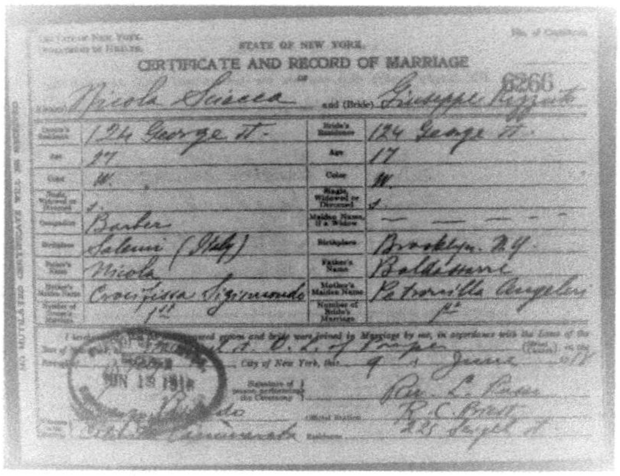

Maria Formica estate notice, *Brooklyn Times Union*, November 3, 1932

Josephine Rizzuto & Nicola Sciacca,
wedding day, 1918

Josephine Rizzuto,
wedding day, 1918

Nicola Sciacca,
wedding day, 1918

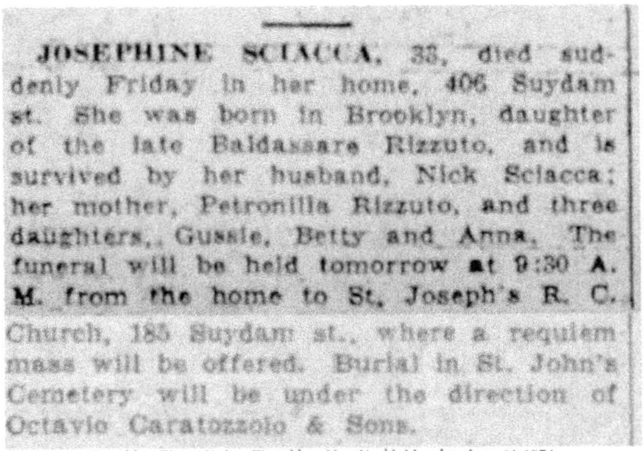

JOSEPHINE SCIACCA, 33, died suddenly Friday in her home, 406 Suydam st. She was born in Brooklyn, daughter of the late Baldassare Rizzuto, and is survived by her husband, Nick Sciacca; her mother, Petronilla Rizzuto, and three daughters, Gussie, Betty and Anna. The funeral will be held tomorrow at 9:30 A. M. from the home to St. Joseph's R. C. Church, 185 Suydam st., where a requiem mass will be offered. Burial in St. John's Cemetery will be under the direction of Octavio Caratozzolo & Sons.

Brooklyn Times Union (Brooklyn, New York), Monday, June 11, 1934

Josephine Sciacca obituary, *Brooklyn Times Union*, June 11, 1934

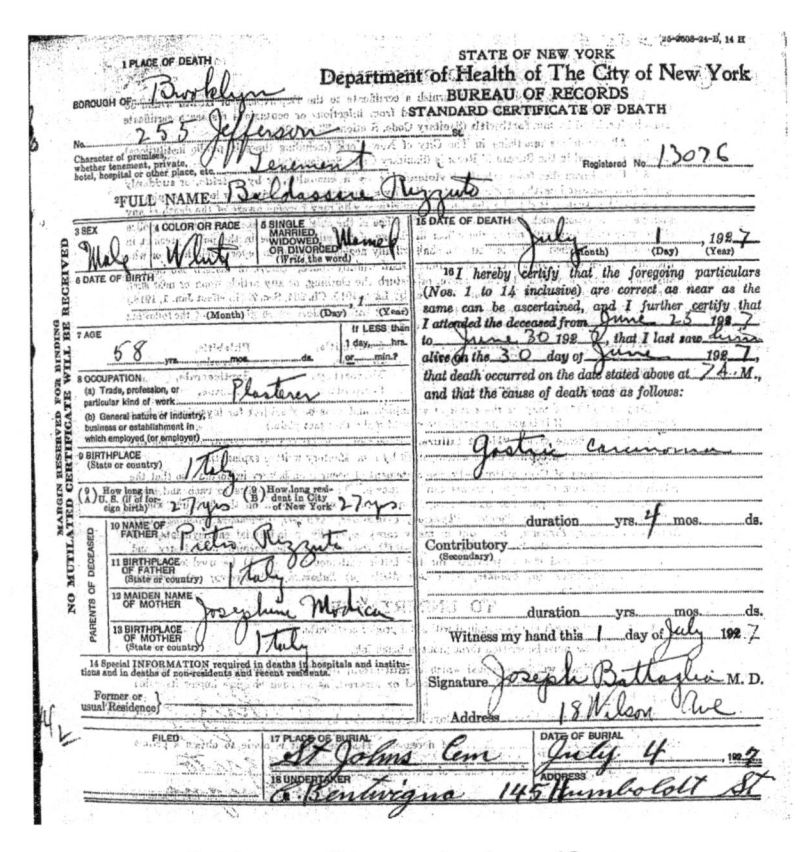

Baldassare Rizzuto death certificate,
July 1, 1927

"What we once enjoyed and deeply loved we can never lose, for all that we love deeply becomes a part of us."

—Helen Keller

The Family Home on Suydam Street

Mama Nonne purchased the home at 406 Suydam Street in Bushwick for $20,000 (the equivalent of $350,000+ today), sometime before 1930, although we are basing this on family stories alone. The three-story brownstone had six apartments and approximately 6,000 square feet. It was a home that saw births, deaths, joy, sorrow, and laughter. Mama Nonne lived there and rented out the other apartments for cash flow. She insisted on cleaning the building herself, scrubbing the flights of mahogany stairs on her hands and knees. Over the years, Mama Nonne's granddaughters would marry and eventually raise their own families there.

The neighborhood was the community where my relatives lived and worked. They had a wonderful life with people walking and talking in the park, playing chess, and drinking espresso. If they closed their eyes, they could be back in the old country. I remember the horse-drawn wagon with the peddler selling his fruits and vegetables. When I close my eyes, a lifetime of memories floods over me, times spent with my cousins and extended family, everyone talking at the same time, and so much laughter. There was always lots of laughter at 406 Suydam Street.

The neighborhood had been undergoing a slow decline, culminating in July of 1977, when much of Bushwick was destroyed by arson and looting during a massive blackout. The family home was eventually sold when my Aunt Gussie's family moved to the Ridgewood neighborhood up the block. Fast forward to 2019 when the Suydam Street property sold for over $1 million. Bushwick has undergone yet another transformation.

St. Joseph's Catholic Church

St. Joseph's Catholic Church at 185 Suydam Street was established in 1921 in Bushwick, to serve the large immigrant population moving to Brooklyn at that time. It would become a very important institution in my family's life. My mother and her sisters were baptized and married there. Their children were baptized and married there. My sister and I were baptized there before we moved to Virginia. When we visited Brooklyn, we attended Mass at St. Joseph's. I remember it as a magnificent building with every adornment, just like a cathedral in Rome.

406 Suydam Street, Bushwick, Brooklyn

The author as a toddler on Suydam Street

The Good Humor Ice Cream truck, Brooklyn

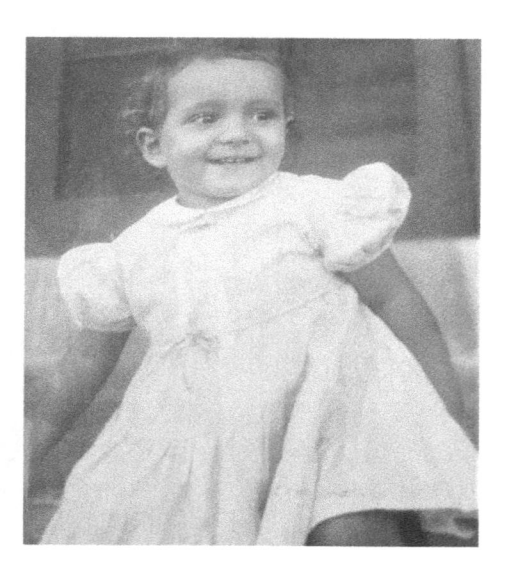

The author as a little girl on Suydam Street

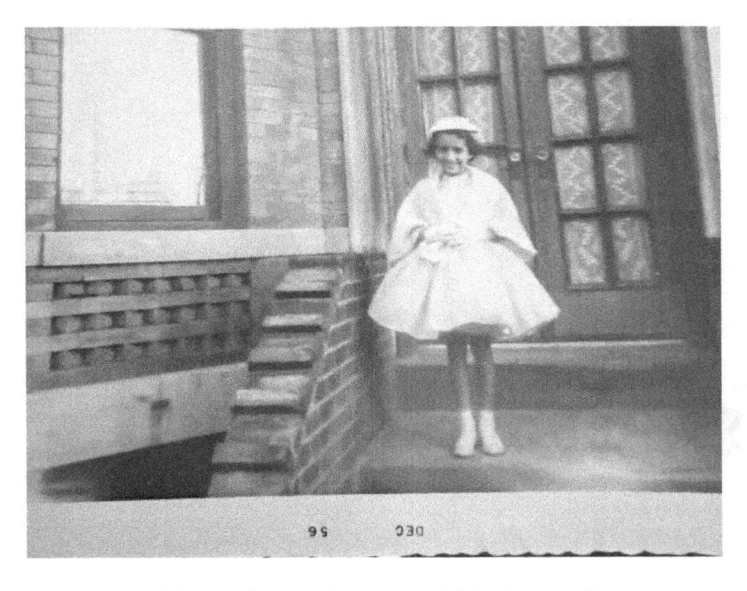

The author at 8 years old in front of
406 Suydam Street

My parents' wedding, St. Joseph's
Church, 1943

Interior of St. Joseph's Catholic
Church

Exterior of St. Joseph's Church

"When a daughter loses a mother, she learns early that human relationships are temporary, that terminations are beyond her control, and her feelings of basic trust and security are shattered. The result? A sense of inner fragility and overriding vulnerability. She discovers she's not immune to unfortunate events, and the fear of subsequent similar losses may become a defining characteristic of her personality."

--Hope Edelman, "Motherless Daughters: The Legacy of Loss"

Motherless Daughters

After reading Hope Edelman's book, I saw parallels between the stories in her book and the lives of my mother and her two sisters. Although I have little firsthand knowledge about their childhoods, Edelman's book recounts the effects a mother's death can have on children's lives. The death of a mother means the loss of the emotional caretaker, and a child has to adapt to everything this means and implies. The loss affects them over time. When a mother dies, a daughter's mourning never completely ends. A mother's death is as close as a daughter will get to experiencing her own death. No matter how old we are, we yearn for a mother's love, reaching for the security and comfort we believe only she can provide in times of illness, transition, and stress. After the loss of their mother, many children experience anxiety, depression, and social withdrawal. In the aftermath of a mother's death, many children feel ashamed about losing their mother and avoid talking about the loss or revealing any anger, depression, guilt or anxiety to their friends and peer group. Many develop a stoic and unemotional coping style in order to feel normal to the outside world.

Adolescence is a period of internal chaos, even without a mother's loss, and my mother and her two sisters were adolescents when they lost their mother at the ages of twelve, fourteen and fifteen. They had to become involuntary mini mothers as my mother became the family cook and Bea and Gussie became the family breadwinners. They learned to associate crying and emotional outbursts with being childish, and their public displays of emotion were rare. As a result of her trauma, my mother became very stoic and rarely displayed her emotions. She could be very disapproving of strong emotional reactions. The death of a mother forces an adolescent to grow up fast and can lead to them becoming closer to their siblings. The sudden death of one's mother teaches children that relationships are impermanent and liable to end at any time. This awareness can dramatically change a child's personality.

Many of the women in my family were relegated to working in sweatshops at various times in their lives—Mama Nonne, her three sisters, her niece Christina, her daughter Josephine, and after Josephine died, her two daughters, Beatrice, and Gussie. I can't imagine what was going through their adolescent brains when they realized their childhood was gone, along with their spiritual caretaker, their mother. My mother and her two sisters were fortunate to have a resilient grandmother in Mama Nonne, who took over the duties of their deceased mother, Josephine, and became the one constant in their lives. Mama Nonne held the family together. Our family was blessed to call her Great Grandmother.

My prayer is that all women who have lost their mothers or daughters know they are not alone.

Anna, Pietronilla, Crucifissa Sciacca,
christening, circa 1924

Your Mother Is Always With You ©

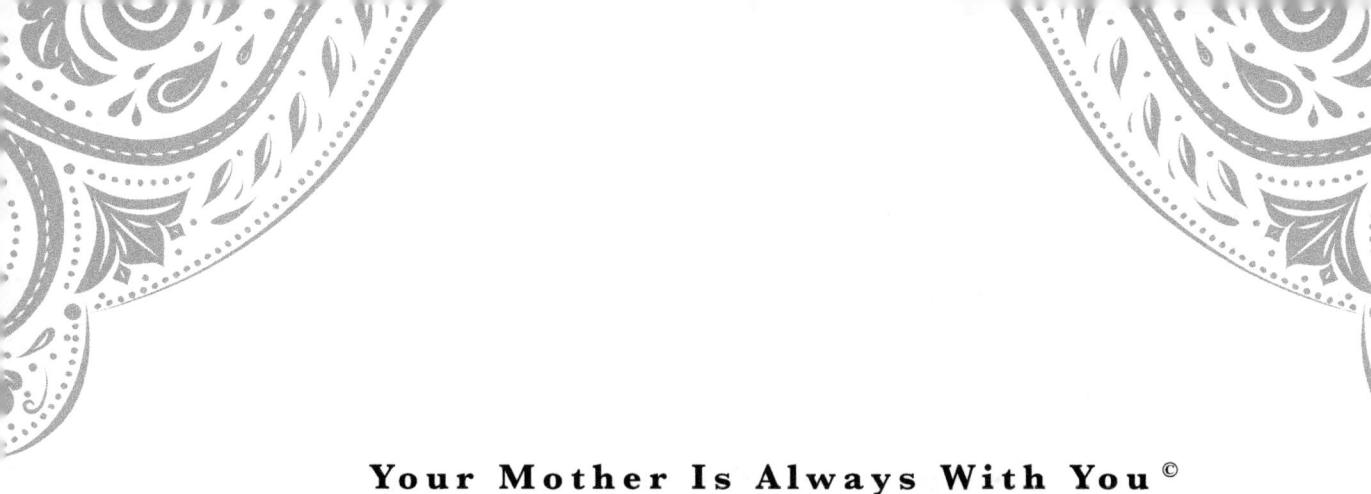

Your Mother is always with you.

She's the whisper of the leaves as you walk down the street.

She's the smell of certain foods you remember, flowers you pick, the fragrance of life itself.

She's the cool hand on your brow when you're not feeling well.

She's your breath in the air on a cold winter's day.

She is the sound of the rain that lulls you to sleep, the colors of a rainbow.

She is Christmas morning.

Your mother lives inside your laughter.

She's the place you come from, your first home.

She's the map you follow with every step you take.

She's your first love, your first friend, even your first enemy.

But nothing on Earth can separate you.

Not time.

Not space.

Not even death.

—Deborah R Culver

"A sister is a gift to the heart, a friend to the spirit and a golden thread to the meaning of life."

—Isadora James

The Belle Sorelle: The Beautiful Sisters

Time passes.

Life happens.

Distance separates.

Children grow up.

Love waxes and wanes.

Men don't do what they're supposed to do.

Hearts break.

Parents die.

Colleagues forget favors.

Careers end.

BUT - Sisters are there, no matter how much time and how many miles are between you.

A girlfriend is never farther away than needing her.

When you have to walk that lonesome valley and you have to walk it by yourself, the women in your life will be on the valley's rim, cheering you on, praying for you, pulling for you, intervening on your behalf, and waiting with open arms at the valley's end.

Sometimes, they will even break the rules and walk beside you or come in and carry you out.

Girlfriends, daughters, granddaughters, daughters-in-law, sisters, sisters-in-law, mothers, grandmothers, aunties, nieces, cousins and extended family all bless our life.

When we began this adventure called womanhood, we had no idea of the incredible joys or sorrows that lay ahead, nor did we know how much we would need each other.

Every day, we need each other still.
--Anonymous

Don't ever forget to share your life with your beautiful sisters.

> "One day we will remember how lucky we were to have known their love, with wonder, not grief."
>
> —**Elizabeth Postle**

Crucifissa Sciacca Dolzani

Crucifissa (Augusta, Gussie) was the first daughter born to Josephine and Nicola Sciacca on February 29, 1919, at 124 George Street. She was named Crucifissa (Crucified Christ) after her father's mother. The family moved to 255 Jefferson Street a few years later, and by 1930, they were living at 406 Suydam Street, where Aunt Gussie and her family would live for many years. After her mother died in 1934, Gussie's schooling ended, and she went to work in a garment factory to help support the family. She married John Dolzani on Sunday, August 29, 1943, at Saint Joseph's Catholic Church. Gussie and John eventually had three children, Joan, Theresa, and Nicholas.

Fond memories of Aunt Gussie abound. She had a wonderful sense of humor, flawless skin, and a great fashion sense. She was always well dressed, even when she was rocking her housecoat and slippers, and she laughed easily and often. She was generous and kind and thoughtful, always looking out for her nieces and nephews, and making everyone feel welcome in her home. I remember how she used to bite her hand the way my father did, an Italian gesture of frustration without yelling or saying anything. She was very kind and sweet to my family. Uncle John was equally kind and calm, and all of us remember the smell of his pipe and how nice and easy-going he was. I remember how he used to hum when he was driving the car.

I still remember the first time Aunt Gussie and Uncle John visited us at our new home in Virginia. She was so excited for my mother and couldn't wait to see the new house. She opened a door in their dining room and almost fell to the ground because the door led outside, but there was no landing. My parents eventually added a porch, but that memory of Aunt Gussie always remained. Even though their visits to Virginia were infrequent, they were always a highlight because they were filled with laughter and fun and sightseeing in Washington, D.C. Aunt Gussie was a kind, sweet, generous soul who seldom got angry.

Josephine Traina

My cousin, Laura, shared memories of Aunt Gussie making polenta for Uncle John, a Tyrolean dish from his family home in northern Italy. She remembered Aunt Gussie allowing them to roller skate in the house, until Cousin Theresa, Gussie's daughter, broke her leg. Theresa remembered coming home with snails from an Italian market on Knickerbocker Avenue, and her mother soaked them and let them crawl around the kitchen. She told a tale of one holiday when the three sisters were in the bathroom smoking and blowing the smoke out the window so their father, Nicola, would not know they smoked.

My sister, Jackie, shared fond memories of how she spent many summers in New York with our cousins. She said Aunt Gussie was the kindest and most generous person she'd ever known. She would even let Jackie borrow her clothes. If our family was in New York on a Friday when Catholics couldn't eat meat, Aunt Gussie often made Milanese, a dish which contained anchovies. She knew Jackie didn't care for it, so she always made sure to pick up a pound of potato salad from Bruno's Deli so Jackie could have that for dinner instead.

I still remember the last time I saw Aunt Gussie. I was visiting with my son, Thomas, then eight months old. Aunt Gussie and Uncle John were having a party at their new home, and I remember her standing over the stove, stirring the sausage and peppers. Their friends, the Paternosters, brought a whole bag of basil from their garden. The aroma is one I will never forget.

Aunt Gussie and Uncle John were so relaxed and calm together, and they had a beautiful marriage that lasted over thirty years. Mama Nonne lived with their family, and they cared for her until her death. Dear Gussie died on November 24, 1974, at 55 years old. My mother said there were hundreds of people at her funeral Mass at St. Patrick's Cathedral, where she worked and was loved by many. She was a beautiful soul. We lost her way too soon.

Gussie, circa age two, undated

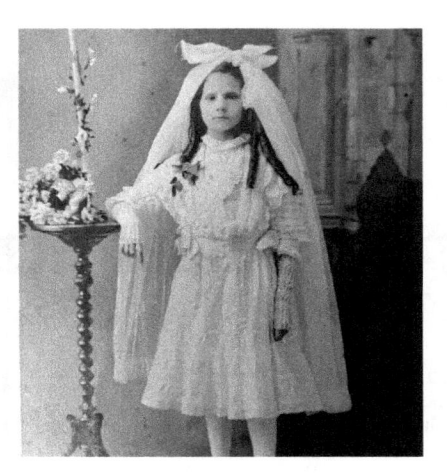

Gussie, First Communion, undated

Gussie Sciacca & John Dolzani, wedding day, 1943

Wedding invitation, August 29, 1943

Gussie, wedding day, 1943

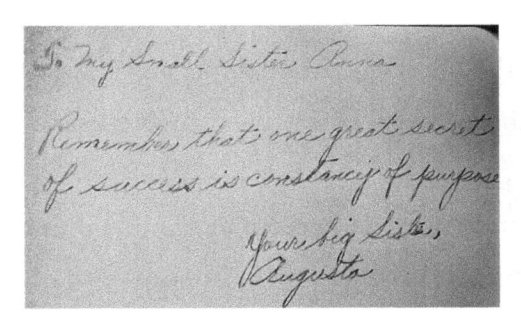

Inscription in her sister Anna's scrapbook, 1937

Best man, my mother, Gussie & John, 1943

"May there be comfort in knowing that
someone so special will never be forgotten."

–Julie Hébert

Pietronilla Sciacca Impellizzeri

Pietronilla (Beatrice) was born on October 4, 1920, the second child of Josephine and Nicola Sciacca. She was named after her mother's mother, our dear Mama Nonne. Her schooling was cut short by the unexpected death of her mother, and she began working at age fourteen in a garment factory, like so many other Sicilian women and girls. One can only imagine the unpleasant working conditions she likely endured as a teenager working in a factory. Out of this tragedy, however, she became an accomplished seamstress and a proud member of the International Ladies' Garment Workers' Union (ILGWU).

Beatrice married the love of her life, Salvatore Impellizzeri, on November 16, 1941, the first sister to wear the beautiful wedding dress sewn by family friend, Emma Borzomati. Bea and Sal raised their four children, Gina, Joanne, Laura, and John at the Suydam Street property owned by Mama Nonne. Aunt Bea was an amazing, resourceful, resilient woman with an indomitable spirit. How she was able to work full time, raise four children, cook fresh, nutritious meals, and keep an immaculate home, was always a mystery to me. I consider her to be a Renaissance woman. Aunt Bea's home was always very orderly. With four children, the old-fashioned roller washing machine ran constantly. My cousins would sit on the fire escape to pin their clothes to the clothesline which hung between the buildings. I remember my cousins ironing their clothes and doing their hair before they went out for the evening. This ritual included lots of hair teasing to get the right bouffant look.

I fondly remember the freedom of being able to walk to the candy store and go out at night and explore. This was exhilarating for me, their country cousin from Virginia. When I was in the presence of Aunt Bea and Uncle Sal, their love was palpable. There were always lots of jokes and laughter and Aunt Bea lovingly called him "Tootie." Once while I was visiting, Aunt Bea and Uncle Sal were taking a bath together, and the laughter coming from the bathroom was hilarious. The entire family was laughing, especially when Uncle Sal sang his own colorful version of the song, "Splish Splash." He was always a jokester, always smiling and accommodating to our family. He was simply the best uncle a niece could ever have, and I adored him.

Aunt Bea and Uncle Sal were truly an inspiration to their family and all who knew them. They raised four children, all of whom had successful marriages, which I attribute to being raised by two people who loved and deeply respected each other. They were my godparents, and they always kept in touch and looked after me, even though we were many miles apart. When I was a single mom raising my four-year-old son and establishing my real estate career, Uncle Sal referred one of his company executives who was being transferred to Georgia. I remember having to leave this client to pick up my son at daycare. Even though I did not close the sale, I will always cherish the memory of my godfather's kindness.

I have fond memories of summers visiting Aunt Bea and Uncle Sal and my cousins, especially at the tiny beach house they rented in Rockaway. Everyone was crammed in, and I remember Aunt Bea sweeping the sand off the floor. There was so much chaos and confusion and laughter and love that it all just seemed magical. The tight living quarters weren't given a second thought. Uncle Sal would take us to Carvel for ice cream. He would also take all the splinters out of my feet after I was repeatedly told to wear shoes instead of going barefoot. On another visit, when I was sleeping in the lower level of their home, I had a nightmare and ran screaming through the house. Uncle Sal told me he slept with a bat by his bed after that. I am so glad my night terror didn't shorten his life.

I always enjoyed hearing funny stories about their beagle, Alfie, who often ran away. He had amusing quirks, like hating umbrellas and graduation gowns. One day, he became gravely ill and was delivered to the vet. Aunt Bea and Uncle Sal were very sad to see their charming beagle go. Imagine their surprise and delight when the vet showed up at their house with a cured dog. I remember one visit when we returned home to find shredded foam everywhere. The dog had torn up several pillows and cushions because he was upset about being left alone. They eventually decided it was time to find Alfie a new home.

Aunt Bea died suddenly on January 17, 2000. She was seventy-nine years old and had lived the longest of the three sisters. Her loss left a huge hole in her family, and much sadness. Uncle Sal was bereft as he told me that Aunt Bea was the love of his life. He told me he did not know how he would live without her. He said, "We were one." I never met two people who were so compatible. They had a loving marriage for almost sixty years.

Josephine Traina

As sad as the loss has been, Aunt Bea's strength, wisdom, and guidance and all the joys and magic memories this beautiful soul left behind help outweigh the sadness. Uncle Sal died September 16, 2016. He was ninety-eight years old.

Beatrice Sciacca,
wedding day, 1941

Salvatore Impellizzeri,
wedding day, 1941

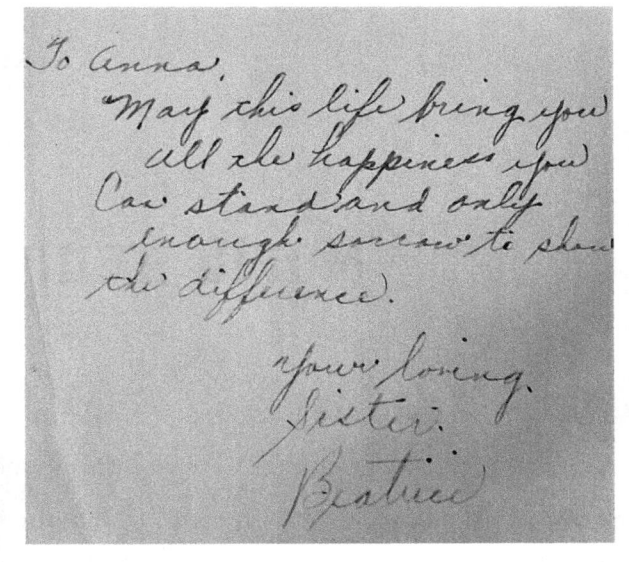

To Anna,
"May this life bring you all the happiness you can stand and only enough sorrow to show the difference."

Your loving Sister,
Beatrice

Inscription in sister Anna's scrapbook, 1937

Gussie, Best man, Carmella,
Beatrice, Salvatore, Anna, 1941

Beatrice & Salvatore, 50th Wedding
Anniversary, 1991

Beatrice,
undated

> "When someone you love becomes a memory,
> the memory becomes a treasure."
>
> —Anonymous

Maria Anna Sciacca Traina

When a mother dies, a daughter grieves, and then life moves on, but missing her, wanting to have just one more conversation, these thoughts stay with me, and especially in springtime. My mother was born in the spring, the earth's birthday; and although she's been gone over thirty years, she comes to me in the form of a butterfly, to let me know she's okay and she wants me to be, too.

Maria Anna Sciacca was born on April 27, 1922, in Brooklyn, the youngest child of Nicola and Josephine Sciacca. Losing her mother at the age of twelve left an indelible mark on my mother's soul. She and her two sisters, Gussie and Bea, had a sisterly bond like no other. Tragedy bound them together, and they would remain close for the rest of their lives. None of the sisters talked much about their childhoods. I feel sure they did not want to burden their children with the trauma they experienced.

As the youngest daughter, my mother had to grow up quickly. She became the family cook and learned how to prepare her mother's recipes. As a result, her cooking was epic. I remember being excited when I reached the top of the hill to our home, and I could smell the delicious food she was preparing. She loved to cook, and she cooked for her family every day, rarely using recipes. She would bake for weeks and deliver Sicilian and Italian treats to her friends at the holidays. Everyone was welcome at her table. I acquired my love of cooking from my mother, and her favorite recipes are in this book for you to share with your family. Sicilian Nonnas are such treasures.

When my mother and father were dating, going to shows at the Paramount Theater was a highlight. Frank Sinatra got his start there, and in December 1942, my parents were in the audience when Jack Benny introduced Sinatra to a crowd of 5,000 fans. The Paramount Theater and Frank Sinatra gave our country hope in dire times, as World War II raged. What a respite from the horrors of war to dance in the aisles while listening to the incredible singer.

Anna married Charles Joseph Traina on July 25, 1943, at St. Joseph's Catholic Church, the second sister to wear the beautiful wedding dress. My parents lived at 406 Suydam Street for a time before my father, who had served in the Office of Strategic Services during WWII, secured a position with the newly formed Central Intelligence Agency in Washington, D.C. My father and many of their neighborhood friends eventually moved their families to Northern Virginia. I was eighteen months old when we left Brooklyn, the only home my mother had ever known. For a short time, all the generations lived at 406 Suydam Street – my parents, my sister Jackie, and me, my Aunt Bea and Uncle Sal and their children, and Aunt Gussie and Uncle John and their children. This must have made Mama Nonne feel so good to see her grandchildren and their families living under one roof and doing so well.

The Borzomati and Sciacca families shared many connections in Brooklyn. My mother grew up with Blanche Borzomati Cascio, her lifelong friend from age ten. Blanche's father owned the print shop where my grandfather worked. My father started his printing career at that print shop, as well. Blanche's mother, Emma, was friends with my grandmother, Josephine. After Josephine tragically died in 1934, Emma was very kind to my mother and her sisters. Years later, she sewed the beautiful wedding dress all three of the Sciacca sisters wore. The connections extended to Blanche's brother, Joseph, who worked as a printer and interpreter during WWII. When my father was getting ready to be shipped out for the D-Day invasion, Joe requested that he come to work with him as a printer in Washington, D.C. Many years later, my father acknowledged that Joe Borzomati had saved his life.

These connections with the Borzomati family followed my parents to Virginia. Many of my mother's Sicilian and Italian friends from the old neighborhood also moved to northern Virginia to begin new lives and jobs. In its own way, it wasn't so different from her own grandparents finding an Italian neighborhood to settle in when they arrived from Sicily. Blanche and her husband Morris also moved to Virginia and lived nearby. They became part of our extended family from Brooklyn. Other families in the entourage included Blanche's brother, Joe and his family, and Nick and Mary Perini. Holiday celebrations with the Borzomatis were always fun. My mother and the Sicilian and Italian entourage of people they had grown up with made the trek to Virginia, but they still kept their Sicilian roots and spoke the language they were raised in.

My mother and father were founding members of Our Lady of Good Counsel Catholic Church in Vienna, Virginia. Their Italian family grew as they gravitated toward each other. The church family

Josephine Traina

became their extended family. My mother and Blanche were the official cooks for the annual spaghetti dinner which raised money for the church.

Like her own mother, Josephine, my mother gave birth to three daughters and named them Jacqueline, Josephine, and Stefani. I'm so grateful she became a grandmother in her mid-forties, when Jackie had her sons, Michael and Tony. My son, Thomas, was born a few years later. She was a wonderful Nana to her three grandsons, and she showered them with love. They loved her dearly and their antics gave her much pleasure. She also had two granddaughters, my daughter Alexis Ann and Stefani's daughter Laura, and a fourth grandson, Steven, who was born the year before she died. My daughter, Alexis, knew her Nana briefly, but, sadly, Stefani's children did not have the opportunity to know their grandmother very well.

I remember my mother listening to her Italian music. When the singer, Jerry Vale, sang the song "Mama," her eyes would fill with tears. She was often very sad. She told me she never got over the loss of her mother. She rarely spoke about her childhood, but I could sense it was filled with many traumas. My mother and her sisters lost their innocence and childhood the day their mother died, but out of the darkness, the three beautiful sisters and their resilience helped them navigate their lives without her.

Blanche's niece, Loretta Cavallo Boyle, recently shared with me her fond memories of the special bond she had with my mother. When Loretta lived on our street for a couple of years, my mother helped her through a very tough time in her life. She was a young mother with two young children, and a husband who was rarely around. She said my mother took care of her and her children and was always helpful and never judgmental. Loretta used to cut and color my mother's hair, and my mother would hold her face in both hands and kiss her. When she closes her eyes, Loretta can still picture my mother, Blanche, me and her playing cards and talking and laughing. Many years later, my parents attended Loretta's daughter's wedding in California.

Aunt Bea's daughter, Laura, shared several fond memories of my mother. She thought it was great that my mother could drive a car. She remembered an Easter egg hunt my mother organized at their first home in Falls Church. She remembered the sleeping arrangements being tight, but loved the games we would play before going to sleep. She loved writing letters to me, and we were pen pals for a very long time. She remembered my father and his jazz records. She always thought he looked like Jerry Lee Lewis. He played the music loud and made us wake up for his delicious pancakes. She remembered going to Virginia and raking leaves, a real treat for a city kid! The burning leaves smelled great. She loved their visits, and loved the trip down to Virginia. The suburban lifestyle was as different for them as the city was for me and my sisters. I am so glad my mother and her sisters felt it was important to keep in close contact despite the miles separating our families.

My mother had many, many friends. She loved cooking, dancing, laughing, and having a good party. She was an excellent bridge player and decent golfer and she bowled, as well. She would cook elaborate Italian dinners for her extended family and friends. Everyone loved Anna. She was gracious and kind and she loved her family dearly.

One of my happiest memories was spending time doing her hair and makeup before she went out for the evening. She had the most beautiful eyes, changing from green to gray. She wasn't a big hugger or kisser, but when I came home from college, I would see her little face in the glass of our front door, and her smile and hugs and kisses were one of my best memories of her and her love.

I am very thankful my parents were able to visit Italy on nine separate occasions, including a visit to Sicily, where they saw relatives. I was able to send them on their first trip because I worked for American Airlines and got round trip tickets for $99 each. Their friends surprised them at Dulles Airport by wishing them a bon voyage.

Blanche and Morris were generous, compassionate, and caring to my parents, even as my mother's Alzheimer's Disease progressed. They always lived a few houses away, even moving with my parents to a new neighborhood in far flung Centreville when the old neighborhood in Vienna was sold and razed for apartments. They were godparents to my sister, Stefani, and my parents were godparents to their daughter, Anna. They visited my parents and were kind friends until the end. Even after my mother died, Blanche would call my father and check in on him. She used to call me and leave a message on my recorder, "Josephine Traina, this is Blanche checking up on you." The Borzomatis and Cascios were very special friends to my family, and I am thankful we had this spiritual connection. The last ten years of my mother's life were increasingly sad for everyone in the family. She was diagnosed as most likely having Alzheimer's Disease, and her decline was quite painful to witness. She died on June 21, 1991. She was sixty-nine years old.

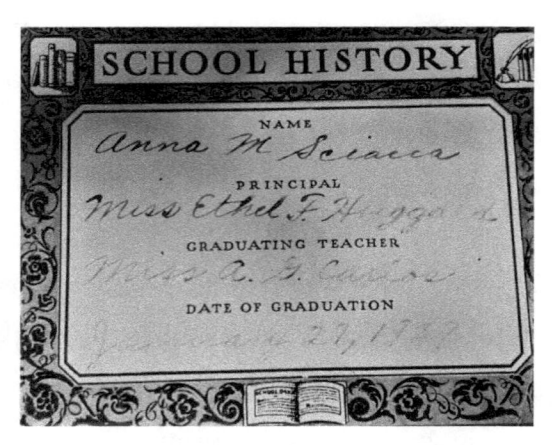

My mother's school certificate, 1937

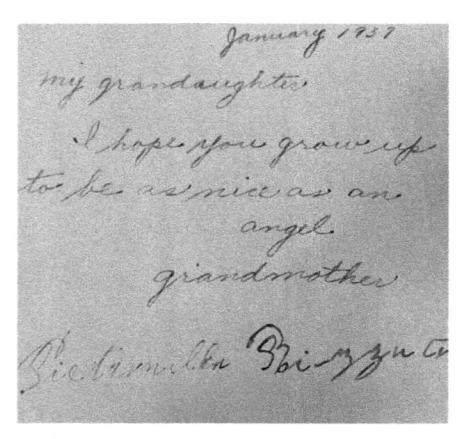

Mama Nonne's inscription in my mother's autograph book, 1937

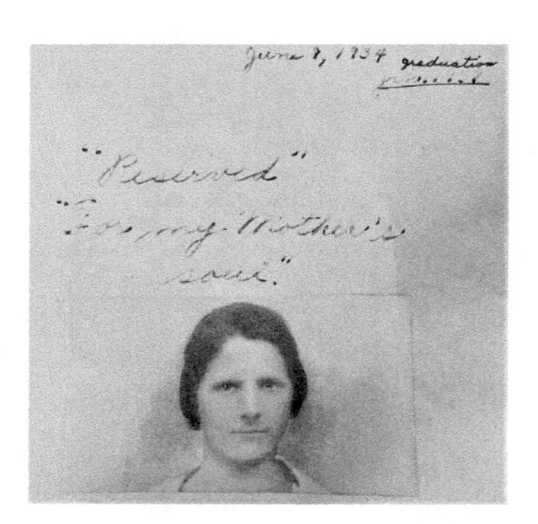

My mother's memory page for her late mother, 1937

My mother's inscription in her autograph book, 1937

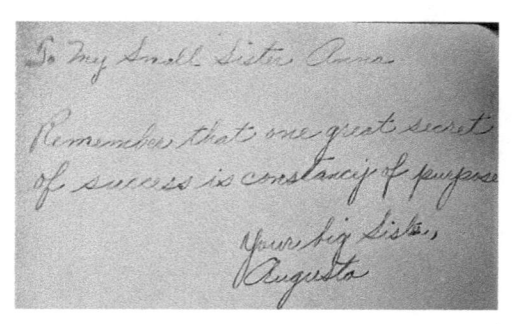

Gussie's inscription in my mother's autograph book, 1937

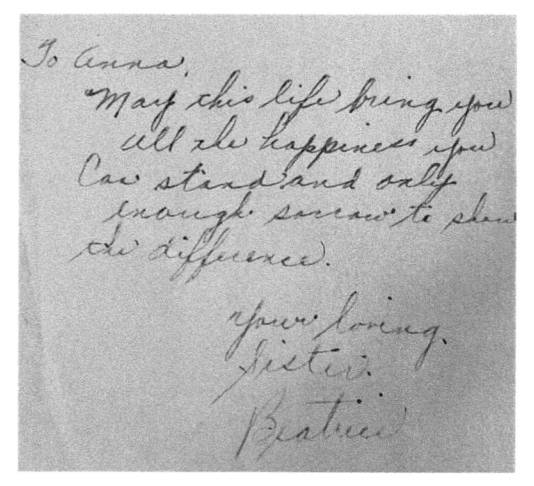

Beatrice's inscription in my mother's autograph book, 1937

My mother, 1941

My mother, circa 1938

My mother, wedding day, 1943

My mother, 16 years old,
Suydam Street, 1938

My mother & father,
wedding day, 1943

Frank Sinatra, Paramount Theater,
Times Square, 1943

Jacqueline, Josephine,
Anna, Stefani, 1980

"In her absence, we will always feel her presence."

Mama Nonne

Mama Nonne means great-grandmother, but she was so much more than that.

Mama Nonne's life was filled with immeasurable loss and self-sacrifice, and she came from a country where famine was an everyday struggle. She lived with this sense of scarcity throughout her life. She was a poor, uneducated, Sicilian immigrant who eventually endured losing her husband, five children, and three sisters. Her entire generation, except for her brother-in-law, had died by 1934. She had no one to share her losses with. Mama Nonne outlived them all. She lost everyone and became the family's matriarch by default. These burdens had to be overwhelming. How especially heartbreaking to have been a motherless child herself, losing her own mother at age ten, and then watching her only daughter die and leave her grandchildren motherless, as well. Despite it all, I believe she must have also felt a sense of pride and happiness as she watched Josephine's children, her beautiful granddaughters, raising their families in the home on Suydam Street.

Mama Nonne remained frugal, even watering down her tomato sauce, the worst no no for an Italian cook. She loved to sit in her rocking chair in the cellar, crocheting and praying. When I close my eyes, I can see her, so peaceful in the warm cocoon of the cellar, with the sounds of the pipes humming. As a child, I had no idea what kind of life she had endured or all the sacrifices she had made so we could have a better life. She lived simply, asking nothing for herself. Her life was spent taking care of her family. Her tiny room was filled with pictures of saints. She stashed money in a pot under her bed and she would give us money for the candy store. Even though we didn't communicate by language, we did communicate with our hearts, and my entire family always felt her love. She was a kind, gentle soul who sacrificed so we could have a better life.

Mama Nonne

When my parents decided to leave New York to move to the Washington, D.C. area for a job opportunity, Mama Nonne encouraged them to go. She helped my parents buy their first automobile and gave them a down payment for their first home in Virginia. I remember our family driving from Virginia and arriving in Brooklyn and seeing Mama Nonne sitting in the window waiting for us to arrive. She looked like an angel with her white hair in a bun. Her beautiful spirit would fill us up. I remember her sitting in a chair in the kitchen, eating a piece of bread and talking to my aunts and uncles in Italian. Everyone was talking at the same time, a family tradition. When I close my eyes, I see the stoop where my cousins and I played handball against the steps. When we entered the building, I remember seeing her name, Rizzuto. I was confused because I never knew her as anything but Mama Nonne. I remember once when our family was getting ready to leave to drive back to Virginia, when Mama Nonne ran across the street and was almost hit by a truck. This tiny angel loved us dearly and did not want to miss saying good-bye. These are memories I will always cherish.

Momma Nonne was deeply religious, with a faith that knew no bounds. This beautiful soul never lost her faith in God, although she had lost all her children, her husband, and her sisters. After so many tragic losses, the only thing she could rely on was her faith. She walked a mile each way to 6:00 a.m. Mass at St. Joseph's every day. Sadly, this daily ritual was taken away late in her life when she was mugged while walking home and left in the street with a broken hip. This beautiful soul who knew only love, sacrifice and caring for her family, was no longer able to walk to her beloved St. Joseph's.

As I walk in Mama Nonne's shoes, it is incomprehensible to think how one human could endure this amount of heartache and grief. I know she must have had a unique relationship with each person she lost, but she had no time for grieving. She had to put her feelings aside because she was the breadwinner and matriarch of the family, and she had to persevere and take care of her three motherless granddaughters. The cumulative grief she endured and survived is a testament to her faith, resilience, courage, and love. The kind, beautiful soul who, despite her own terrible losses, remained the backbone of our family, and bore these burdens selflessly. All she had was her strong faith and hope that her granddaughters and their children would have a better life. This persistence of character was passed down to me, one of the many blessings this beautiful soul left to me, and I now pass all these life lessons on to my family.

At the end of her life, Mama Nonne was bedridden in her small room where my Aunt Gussie took care of her until the day she died. One day she was attending to Mama Nonne when I heard her call out for her Mama. Aunt Gussie said, "When we are born, we cry for our Mama, and when we are dying at the end, we cry for her then, too." So true.

Josephine Traina

When Mama Nonne arrived in America in 1900, the average life expectancy for a man was forty-four and for a woman forty-six. Before she died, she requested to be buried in a nun's habit. When she died, three months shy of her 99th birthday, on January 18, 1968, her granddaughters granted her final wish. Her funeral service was held at St. Joseph's, where she had attended the funerals of her husband and daughter. Mama Nonne was buried in St. John's Cemetery, next to Josephine and her beloved Baldassare. Her life was a journey filled with tragedy and triumph. Old places have souls. Suydam Street was filled with the souls of many family members and the love they shared. Their legacy lives on in their children, grandchildren, great-grandchildren, and great-great-grandchildren.

Mama Nonne and Baldassare knew that real estate was an investment which holds its value over time, as true in the 1920s as it is today. I can feel what they were experiencing, the fear of what might happen next, the uncertainty of wondering if you would survive the downturns, the turbulent years. They understood that owning where you lived meant you would always have a roof over your head. These Sicilian immigrants were self-made, self-taught, and very forward thinking.

When Mama Nonne made the decision to leave Sicily and boarded the ship for America, she was beginning her journey to fulfill a lifelong wish to create a family and provide a safe place for them to live. Her fulfilled dream lives on in all of us. I can feel Mama Nonne smiling down on me. She never gave up hope about her life, for she had succeeded at what she set out to do. She built a better life for herself and future generations. She accomplished this in her lifetime for her family.

Josephine, Baldassare, Mama Nonne, Pietro, circa 1915

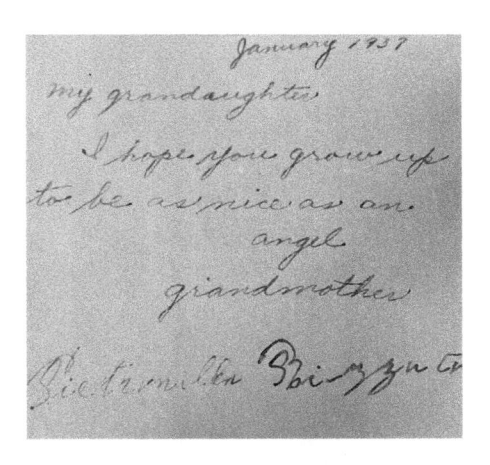

Inscription in granddaughter Anna's scrapbook, 1937

Mama Nonne & great-granddaughter, Gina, circa 1961

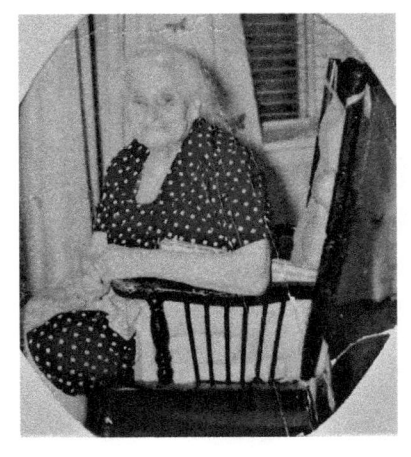

Mama Nonne's funeral card, 1968

Mama Nonne, undated

"Your pain didn't start with you, but it can end with you."
—Stephanie M. Hutchins

Epilogue

"You don't know who you are until you find out where you came from." My son's wise words inspired me to search deeply into how our family became Americans. This journey of self-discovery has been a cathartic, humbling, and worthwhile adventure.

During this quest to find my roots, I discovered my great-grandparents' lives paralleled mine in important ways, which is why their story resonated with me. My own real estate career and my great-grandparent's forays into real estate connect me to them. Threads running through this tale are being free to own your own home or business, building a better life for the family, being safe and secure, and having faith and hope all will be well. I feel their spirit guided me to persevere through the darkest of days. I knew I would survive and thrive in building a better life for myself and my family, and like them, I worked tirelessly toward these goals.

My great-grandparents craved freedom without limitations on what they could achieve. They worked tirelessly to move their family up in the world by buying one property after another. During my career, I was self-employed, and like my great-grandparents, wanted to run my own business and not be in servitude like they were in the old country. I, too, followed their lead, buying one property after another to build a legacy for my family. They were entrepreneurs with big dreams, and I, too, had the entrepreneurial spirit, wanting to be accountable to no one but myself. We both sacrificed greatly. There were always scarcity and burdens and a constant desire never to be controlled by anyone or anything. They owned and managed four properties at one time. I, too, had four houses, and the struggle was real for both of us. Depressions, recessions, inflation, and unemployment are all factors which make investing in real estate a risky and challenging proposition, not for the faint of heart.

I acquired many material possessions in my life, including cars and houses, but even though I lived in abundance, a scarcity mindset persisted. A poverty consciousness passed down to me propelled me to

Josephine Traina

repeat the same gut-wrenching fears of being homeless and losing everything. I worried I wouldn't be able to provide for my family. I carried these burdens and suffered for much of my life. Despite my success, I looked for what was missing instead of being grateful for my accomplishments. I lived in lack instead of in abundance, constantly fearing there would never be enough, and I would never be enough. I needed to confront the limiting beliefs and unconscious patterns I was running in my own life. I needed to examine all the rules I had made for myself to be happy. We are an accumulation of our ancestors, great-grandparents, grandparents, and parents. I had been living my life through filters I had not chosen, the patterns of those who came before me. They were a part of me, and they often affected how I felt and reacted to situations. Whose voice was I hearing? Was it me or all the patterns and filters through which I was viewing my life?

I've come to understand that repeating past patterns in an unconscious attempt to release unresolved trauma only keeps the problems recycling and continuing to repeat. The only way to remove the shackles of my past was to become aware of the patterns I was running, and to acknowledge these may not have been mine. They didn't start with me. I had a habit of unconsciously carrying someone else's pain and burdens. By putting this on paper, I can release the unresolved pain and trauma that never belonged to me. I now realize this mindset of sacrifice, lack, and control did not serve me. They were filters I viewed my life through. Someone once said that once you write about a memory, you don't have to carry it around. I now put down the "invisible suitcase" which kept me captive my whole life.

Our ancestral grandfathers and grandmothers, mothers, fathers, aunts, and uncles were pioneers and risk takers. They sacrificed personal comfort to provide a better life for their families. They didn't view it as a sacrifice but did it willingly and gladly. The life lessons these souls taught me were the importance of having a solid work ethic and a strong sense of responsibility, along with self-respect, perseverance, resilience, and love of family. This tale is my opportunity to pass along their legacy to my children, grandchildren, great-grandchildren, and my entire family. And I have learned in every dark cloud, there is a blessing, even though life is never easy or fair. I want my family to know that in spite of life's trials and tribulations, they have been given gifts of faith, hope, perseverance, and resilience from those who came before them. Those solid Sicilian traits are part of each of us.

Researching this book has given me insight into the women like Mama Nonne, who have been invisible for too long. The culture of Sicilian and Italian women taught them to be submissive and to live in the shadows of a patriarchal society. By casting a light on their considerable accomplishments and sacrifices, I hope to give them a place of honor they richly deserve. My Mom, Aunt Gussie, and Aunt Bea were excellent role models. They lost their innocence and childhood when their mother died and had to learn to navigate life without a mother. This event brought them even closer together. All of them left solid matriarchal values they passed down to us, a love of cooking, family, kindness, gentleness, and generosity of spirit.

Anything I do in my life will never be even a tiny portion of what my great-grandparents sacrificed so we would have a better life. May this Sicilian immigrant tale of sacrifice, lack, and control heal other hearts and souls. If you have been unconsciously carrying burdens on your shoulders, it is time to put that suitcase down. May you heal in every way from any harmful filters through which you have lived your own life, what you received without realizing it, what was never yours to begin with.

"A great soul serves everyone all the time. A great soul never dies. It brings us together again and again."

—Maya Angelou

Souls of the Dearly Departed: Sicilian Names & How They Were Passed On

I never understood why so many people in my family had the same names. I learned there was a longstanding practice in Sicilian and Italian culture to name children after relatives in a particular way and following a particular order, beginning with the father's parents. The following explains the derivation of some of the names on my mother's side of the family.

PIETRONILLA

Pietronilla Angeleri (Mama Nonne) was the daughter of Baldassare & Leonarda Angeleri.

1. Pietronilla Sciacca Impellizzeri - Beatrice (daughter of Josephine Rizzuto Sciacca & Nicola Sciacca) - named after her grandmother, Mama Nonne.

PIETRO

Baldassare Rizzuto was the son of Pietro Rizzuto & Giuseppa Monica Rizzuto.

1. Pietro Rizzuto (son of Mama Nonne & Baldassare Rizzuto; he died at 15 months) - named after Baldassare's father (Pietro Rizzuto).
2. Pietro Rizzuto (son of Mama Nonne & Baldassare Rizzuto; he died at age 5) - named after Baldassare's father (Pietro Rizzuto).

Josephine Traina

JOSEPHINE

Giuseppa Monica Rizzuto - Baldassare Rizzuto's mother.

1. Josephine Rizzuto Sciacca (daughter of Mama Nonne & Baldassare Rizzuto) - named after Baldassare's mother (Giuseppa Monica Rizzuto).
2. Josephine Traina (daughter of Maria Anna Sciacca Traina & Charles Traina) - named after Anna's mother (Josephine Rizzuto Sciacca).

CRUCIFISSA

1. Crucifissa Sciacca (crucified Christ) - Nicola Sciacca's mother.
2. Crucifissa Sciacca - Augustus, Gussie (daughter of Josephine Rizzuto Sciacca & Nicola Sciacca) - named after Nicola's mother (Crucifissa Sciacca).

MARIA

1. Maria Angeleri was Mama Nonne's sister.
2. Maria Anna Sciacca Traina (daughter of Josephine Rizzuto Sciacca & Nicola Sciacca) - named after Josephine's aunt (Maria Angeleri).

NICHOLAS

1. Nicola Sciacca (maternal grandfather).
2. Nicholas Dolzani (son of Crucifissa Sciacca Dolzani & John Dolzani) - named after Nicola Sciacca.

FAMILY TREE

Baldassare & Leonarda (Renda) Angeleri ←→ Pietro & Giuseppina (Modica) Rizzuto

- Giuseppina *(1859-1928)*
- Angela *(1860-1908)*
- Maria *(1866-1932)*
- Pietronilla *(1870-1968)*

- Melchiore *(1851-1940)*
- Antonina *(1858-?)*
- Nicolo *(1862-?)*
- Giuseppe *(1868-?)*
- Baldassare *(1865 or 1869-1927)*

↓

Baldassare & Pietronilla Rizzuto *married 1899*

- Josephine *(1900-1934)*
- Pietro *(1902-1904)*
- Pietro *(1910-?)*
- 2 others
  - Baldassare *(1865 or 1869-1927)*
  - Pietronilla *(1870-1968)*

↓

Josephine & Nicola Sciacca *married 1918*

- Crucifissa *(1919-1974)*
- Pietronilla *(1920-2000)*
- Maria Anna *(1922-1991)*
  - Josephine *(1900-1934)*
  - Nicola *(1890-1977)*

Crucifissa & John Dolzani
married 1943
- Joan
- Theresa
- Nicholas
  - Crucifissa *(1919-1974)*
  - John *(1917-1990)*

Beatrice & Salvatore Impellizzeri
married 1941
- Gina
- Joanne
- Laura
- John
  - Beatrice *(1920-2000)*
  - Salvatore *(1918-2016)*

Anna & Charles Traina
married 1943
- Jacqueline
- Josephine
- Stefani
  - Anna *(1922-1991)*
  - Charles *(1919-2018)*

"Sicilians build things like they will live forever and eat like they will die tomorrow."

--Plato

La Cucina: Cooking is a Gesture of Love

The kitchen, "la cucina," is an entire world, and its rituals are where the whole family comes together. Everything I learned about the love of cooking came from my mother. For Sicilians and Italians, cooking is a gesture of love. Sicilian and Italian immigrants brought their love of food and cooking with them across the Atlantic Ocean and through the doors of Ellis Island. They also brought their culture centered around family, a spirit of place, the importance of belonging, and a strong identity which included their rich history and understanding of art and music.

Sicily is known for its artichokes, anchovies, fresh mint, gelato, and citrus produce. Sicilian cuisine is savory, spicy and flavorful and reflects the numerous cultural influences of the many different groups who ruled the island. The Arab influence is noticeable in spicy dishes which include eggplant, olive oil, pine nuts, capers, and tomatoes.

Desserts are another Sicilian specialty. The cannoli, the king of Sicilian sweets, is extremely sweet, creamy, and rich, and fills your mouth with voluptuousness. Its contents are a rich burst of textures and distinct tastes, and pair well with their crispy, aromatic shell, which we refer to as "scorza," exactly like the skin of citrus fruits. They are not a treat for the faint of heart.

The ritual of sitting at the table and breaking bread with the family is a gift which was passed on to me, and I now pass it on to the next generations. Cooking is a labor of love for me, a gift, and a means of imparting the knowledge of "la cucina" to others. I was raised this way, cooking and entertaining as my mother and her sisters did. The greatest joy, happiness and memories are of my mother's epic cooking, which she passed on to me and my sisters. You will never leave a Sicilian home hungry, as food is our way of connecting with people. From the moment you step in the door, you will be served tons of food, as though you were a small army. Don't be surprised to hear the word "Mangia!" (Eat!) a good bit. Afterwards we will drop you off where you are staying and spoil you until you are officially out of our care.

Josephine Traina

The recipes included here are family favorites from the matriarchal side of my family. Many of these are not exact, as that's how we cook. It is with love that I share some favorite recipes of The Belle Sorelle. When I cook one of my mother's recipes, my heart is full, and I am thankful to be a Sicilian Italian. Buon Appetito!

MY ITALIAN WEDDING SOUP

This soup is warm and comforting and filled with tender bison meatballs, veggies, and acini de pepe. This classic Italian soup will become an instant family favorite!

INGREDIENTS

8 ounces ground bison

8 ounces ground hot Italian sausage (casings removed)

1/4 cup breadcrumbs

1 large egg

1 tablespoon Italian seasoning

1 tablespoon olive oil

1/4 cup onion (chopped)

3 large carrots (chopped)

2 stalks celery (chopped)

3 garlic cloves (minced)

10 cups chicken stock

1/2 cup uncooked acini di pepe pasta (orzo will also work)

4 cups spinach (chopped)

1/2 cup parmesan cheese

salt and pepper

PREPARATION

In a medium-sized mixing bowl, add the ground bison, sausage, breadcrumbs, egg, Italian seasoning, and salt and pepper. Stir until combined. Roll into one-inch meatballs, making about 25-30. Set aside.

Add the olive oil, onion, carrots, celery, and garlic to a large pot. Cook for 2-3 minutes or until tender. Add the chicken stock, pasta, and meatballs and bring to a boil. Reduce heat to a simmer and cook for about 10 minutes or until the meatballs are cooked through and pasta is tender. Stir in the spinach and allow it to wilt. Season with salt and pepper and top with freshly grated parmesan cheese.

Josephine Traina

What are acini di pepe? The name in Italian means "seeds of pepper." They are known as a symbol for fertility and that is why they are used in Italian wedding soup. They are also sometimes referred to as pastina, (Italian for "tiny dough") but some pasta makers distinguish pastina as smaller than acini di pepe.

MY MOM'S PASTA FAGIOLI

INGREDIENTS

1 pound dried lima beans

1 ham hock bone

1/4 cup olive oil

2 small cloves garlic, finely chopped

1/2 can tomato paste

1 cup elbow macaroni

salt and pepper

PREPARATION

Soak beans overnight. Drain and place beans and ham hock bone in 3 1/2 quarts of cold water. Cover and cook for 1 1/2 hours.

In a medium frying pan sauté the garlic in olive oil. Stir in the tomato paste. Simmer for ten minutes, stirring occasionally. Add the sauce to the beans with a dash of salt and pepper. Add more water if the soup is too thick. Remove ham hock and simmer for two hours until beans are cooked.

Cook macaroni separately for 10 to 12 minutes. Add to the soup and serve.

Josephine Traina

AUNT BEA'S VEGETABLE SOUP

INGREDIENTS

2 tablespoons olive oil

1 medium (sweet) onion, diced

1 clove garlic, minced

2 tablespoons tomato paste

3 stalks chopped celery

2 carrots, sliced

2 potatoes, diced

1/2 lb. green beans

1 package frozen peas

PREPARATION

Place olive oil in a pot and add onion and garlic. Sauté for 5 minutes. Add the tomato paste diluted in one cup of water. Cook for 5 minutes. Add 4 cups of water and celery, carrots, potatoes and cook for 15 minutes. Add the green beans and peas. Season to taste. Add more water if needed.

Variation: To make Vegetable Bean soup, add one can of Progresso cannellini beans.

MY MOM'S ANDY BOY BROCCOLI

My Mom used to make this on cold rainy days.

INGREDIENTS

2 medium cloves garlic

salt

¾ pound broccoli florets

2 tablespoons extra virgin olive oil

freshly ground black pepper

1 teaspoon Better Than Bouillon

6 ounces short tubular pasta, or other dried small pasta shape for soup, such as ditalini or small shells

PREPARATION

Fill a pot with water that will accommodate the broccoli and place over high heat. Peel and finely chop the garlic. When the water boils, add 1 teaspoon salt and add the broccoli. After the water comes back to a boil, cook until tender, about 5 minutes. Drain the broccoli and set aside.

Put the garlic and olive oil in a 4- to 6-quart soup pot and place over medium-high heat. After the garlic begins to sizzle, add the cooked broccoli. Season with pepper and lightly with salt and sauté for about 5 minutes. Stir periodically with a wooden spoon, using it to mash the broccoli into small pieces. When the broccoli has finished sautéing, add 4 cups water and the Better than Bouillon and raise the heat to high. When the water begins boiling, add the pasta and cover and cook over medium heat until the pasta is al dente.

Josephine Traina

MY MARINARA SAUCE

Yield: 3½ cups, enough for 1 pound of pasta

INGREDIENTS

1 28-ounce can whole San Marzano tomatoes

1/4 cup extra virgin olive oil

7 garlic cloves, peeled and slivered

1 small dried whole chili, or pinch crushed red pepper flakes

1 teaspoon kosher salt

1 large fresh basil sprig, or ¼ teaspoon dried oregano, more to taste.

PREPARATION

Step 1

Pour tomatoes into a large bowl and crush with your hands. Pour 1 cup water into the can and slosh it around to get tomato juices. Reserve.

Step 2

In a large skillet (do not use a deep pot) over medium heat, heat the oil. When it is hot, add garlic.

Step 3

As soon as garlic is sizzling (do not let it brown), add the tomatoes, then the reserved tomato water. Add whole chili or red pepper flakes, oregano (if using) and salt. Stir.

Step 4

Place basil sprig, including stem, on the surface (like a flower). Let it wilt, then submerge in sauce. Simmer sauce until thickened and oil on surface is a deep orange, about 15 minutes. (If using oregano, taste sauce after 10 minutes of simmering, adding more salt and oregano as needed.) Discard basil and chili (if using).

AUNT GUSSIE'S SAINT JOSEPH'S DAY RECIPE - PASTA MILANESE

On Fridays, when Catholics were not allowed to eat meat, this was a family favorite.

Saint Joseph is the patron saint of Sicily. Thanks are given to St. Joseph for preventing famine in Sicily in the Middle Ages. Every year on March 19th, everyone gathers to prepare a large feast to honor him. Foods are traditionally served with breadcrumbs consisting of Sicilian breading and parmigiano Reggiano sprinkled on top to represent saw dust, since Joseph was a carpenter.

INGREDIENTS

1/4 cup extra virgin olive oil

1 bulb fennel, diced

2 onions, diced

2 garlic cloves, minced

4 anchovy filets

2 14 1/2 oz. cans diced tomatoes

1 28 oz can of San Marzano tomatoes

1 tablespoon sugar

1/4 cup tomato paste

1 teaspoon fennel seed toasted, ground

4 large fresh basil leaves, torn

1/2 teaspoon oregano or (leaves from 2 large sprigs)

1 teaspoon crushed red pepper flakes

1 pound spaghetti or bucatini

PREPARATION

In a large saucepan, heat the olive oil. Add the fennel and onions and cook until browned and caramelized, stirring occasionally. Add the garlic and cook briefly. Stir in the anchovies and cook for a couple of minutes. Add the diced tomatoes and the can of San Marzano tomatoes, crushing them with your hands or a fork. Add the sugar, tomato paste, ground fennel, basil, oregano, and red pepper flakes. Simmer the sauce for 1 hour, stirring occasionally.

In a large pot, cook the pasta, (reserve 1 cup of pasta water) and drain.

Combine some of the sauce with the pasta. If the sauce is thicker than you like, add the reserved pasta water until you get the consistency desired.

Josephine Traina

MY MOM'S PESTO

INGREDIENTS

1 cup fresh basil

1/2 cup parsley

2 cloves garlic, minced

1/2 cup Pecorino Romano cheese

1 cup extra virgin olive oil

1 cup pine nuts or walnuts

PREPARATION

Add all the ingredients in a food processor and blend until thoroughly combined.

Serve over pasta and add Pecorino Romano cheese.

MY CHICKEN PARMIGIANA

INGREDIENTS

1 lb. boneless chicken cutlets

Sliced mozzarella cheese

Marinara sauce

Breadcrumbs

1 egg, lightly beaten

Flour

Grated parmesan cheese

Salt and pepper to taste

PREPARATION

Tenderize the chicken cutlets until thin. Dip cutlets in the beaten egg, then in flour, then in the egg again, and finally in breadcrumbs seasoned with salt pepper and grated cheese. Fry in olive oil until golden brown.

In a glass Pyrex dish, put some marinara sauce down on the bottom to keep the chicken from sticking. Place cooked chicken cutlets in the dish and cover with more sauce. Top with slices of thin mozzarella cheese and bake at 350 for about 20 minutes and/or until the cheese is melted.

Josephine Traina

MY STUFFED SHELLS WITH CHEESE OR MEAT

INGREDIENTS

6 tablespoons extra virgin olive oil

6 cloves garlic, peeled and crushed

6 cans Cento Certified San Marzano Tomatoes (28 oz) crushed

1 teaspoon sea salt

1/2 teaspoon crushed red pepper

1 lb. jumbo shells

1 lb. ricotta cheese, drained

1 lb. mozzarella cheese, 12 oz cut into 1/4 inch cubes, 4 oz shredded

2 cups grated Parmigiano-Reggiano or Grana Padano cheese

3 tbsp fresh Italian parsley

1 large egg

PREPARATION

Preheat the oven to 400°F. Bring a large pot of salted water to a boil for pasta.

In a Dutch oven, heat olive oil over medium heat and sauté garlic until edges are golden, about 2 minutes. Add tomatoes, slosh out tomato can with 1 cup hot water and add to pot. Stir in salt, red pepper and oregano and bring to a rapid simmer. Cook uncovered until thickened, about 20 minutes.
Add shells to boiling pasta water and cook until al dente, then drain and separate onto sheet trays to avoid sticking.

In a bowl, stir together ricotta, cubed mozzarella, 1 cup grated cheese, parsley and egg.
Mix the remaining cheeses in a separate bowl and set aside.
Spread 2 cups of sauce onto the bottom of a 15x10 inch baking dish.
Fill the shells, dividing the filling evenly, and arrange in one layer in the baking dish. Generously top with more sauce and add the remaining cheese and cover the pan with foil.
Bake until bubbly, about 25-30 minutes. Remove the foil and bake until the cheese is golden, about 5 to 10 more minutes. Serves 6.

VARIATION: JUMBO SHELLS STUFFED WITH BISON AND HOT ITALIAN SAUSAGE

Mix 1 lb. ground bison and 4 links of hot Italian sausage removed from the casing.

Sauté crushed garlic in olive oil and add the bison, sausage, and red pepper flakes until cooked through.

Stuff shells with the meat mixture.

Josephine Traina

MY BISON BOLOGNESE

INGREDIENTS

3 tablespoons olive oil, plus more to finish

1 pound ground bison

1 medium carrot, finely chopped

1/2 red onion, chopped

2 cloves garlic, smashed and peeled

1 teaspoon kosher salt, plus more for the pasta water

1 cup dry white wine

1 28-ounce can whole San Marzano tomatoes, crushed by hand

1 3-inch piece Parmesan cheese rind

2 stems fresh basil

1 pound pappardelle pasta

1 cup freshly grated Parmigiano-Reggiano cheese, plus more to serve

2 tablespoons unsalted butter

1 cup whipping cream

PREPARATION

Heat a medium Dutch oven over medium-high heat. Add the olive oil and the ground bison.

Cook, breaking apart the meat into very small pieces with a wooden spoon until the meat is lightly browned, about 8 minutes. Add the carrot, red onion and garlic to the pan and stir to combine. Season with 1 teaspoon salt and cook for 3 minutes or until the vegetables are soft and fragrant. Deglaze the pan with the white wine, scraping up the brown bits from the bottom of the pan with a wooden spoon. Simmer for 5 minutes or until almost completely reduced. Stir in the hand-crushed tomatoes and nestle in the Parmesan rind and basil. Season with the remaining salt.

Reduce the heat to medium and simmer the sauce, stirring occasionally for 25 minutes. Add whipping cream.

In the meantime, bring a large pot of water to a boil over high heat. Season generously with salt.

Add the pasta to the water and cook for 2 minutes less than directed, about 6 minutes. Using tongs, add the pasta directly from the pasta water to the sauce. Add the Parmigiano-Reggiano cheese directly to the bare pasta, along with the butter. Toss the pasta with the sauce to coat, thinning as needed with the pasta water to ensure it clings to the pasta. Serve drizzled with more olive oil and sprinkled with more Parmigiano-Reggiano cheese if desired.

Josephine Traina

MY OVEN BAKED BISON MEATBALLS

INGREDIENTS

1 lb. ground bison

1/4 cup bell pepper of choice, finely chopped

1/2 small onion, finely chopped

1 egg, lightly beaten

3 garlic cloves, minced

2 tablespoons fresh parsley, chopped

1 teaspoon oregano

1/2 teaspoon sea salt plus more to taste

1/2 teaspoon black pepper plus more to taste

1/4 teaspoon red crushed pepper, optional

PREPARATION

Preheat the oven to 400°F.

Line a baking sheet with a silicone baking mat or aluminum foil.

In a large bowl, combine all the ingredients. Mix until well-incorporated.

Form 1 1/2-inch meatballs (about two tablespoons) and place onto the prepared baking sheet. Repeat until all the meat is used.

Bake for 15 minutes, turning meatballs over halfway through.

Enjoy with your favorite sauce or as is!

MY MOM'S SPIEDINI (ITALIAN KEBABS)

INGREDIENTS

1 pound beef (top round), thinly sliced & pounded very thin

1 sweet onion, cut in quarters and separated into layers

Extra virgin olive oil

Bay leaves

Breadcrumbs seasoned with pepper, salt, grated cheese, fresh parsley

PREPARATION

Brush a slice of beef with oil. Add a small amount of breadcrumbs. Roll up the beef and place on a skewer, adding a bay leaf and a slice of onion between each roll. Continue until you have used all the beef.

Drizzle each skewer with olive oil and broil or grill until the meat is cooked through.

Josephine Traina

MY MOM'S EGGPLANT PARMESAN

INGREDIENTS

2 or 3 egg plants (if using small ones, 4 or 5)

4 tablespoons olive oil

2 eggs

garlic powder

oregano

basil

salt & pepper

2 cups seasoned breadcrumbs

Grated Parmesan cheese

Dried parsley

Marinara Sauce

Shredded mozzarella cheese

PREPARATION

In a medium bowl, combine the eggs, olive oil, garlic powder, oregano, pepper and salt. Mix well.

Peel and slice the eggplant. Pour salt on a cookie sheet. Lay eggplant slices on the salted surface. Pour more salt over the eggplant slices. Let sit at room temperature for 1 hour. Remove and rinse off all salt with running water. Dry pieces on paper towels to remove excess moisture. Set aside.

In a large bowl, mix seasoned breadcrumbs, dried parsley, black pepper and grated parmesan cheese. 65% breadcrumbs, 35% parmesan cheese. Mix it up.

Dip eggplant pieces in the egg mixture, then transfer to the breadcrumbs and coat each piece.

Preheat the oven to 375 degrees.

Place eggplant pieces on a non-stick cookie sheet (pre-spray with spray olive oil).

Bake at 375 for 20 minutes, turn them over, and bake for another 20 minutes. Remove from the oven.

Heat oven to 400 degrees.

Spray your glass or metal pan with olive oil and spread your first layer of marinara sauce.

Add the first layer of eggplant. Add sauce and shredded mozzarella. Repeat for 2 or 3 layers. When you get to the top layer, add the shredded mozzarella and add freshly grated parmesan, dried parsley, and black pepper. Use a good amount of freshly grated parmesan.

Bake in at 400 degrees for 20-25 minutes, keeping an eye on it. Center rack. When cheese starts to brown, remove from the oven, and let it rest.

Josephine Traina

AUNT BEA'S CHICKEN WITH ARTICHOKES

INGREDIENTS

Chicken cutlets (boneless)

Flour (seasoned with salt and pepper)

1/2 package frozen artichokes hearts cut in half lengthwise

Garlic to taste

Juice of one lemon

1/2 cup white wine

1/2 cup chicken broth

PREPARATION

Dredge the chicken in flour, shaking off the excess.

Brown in olive oil until golden brown. Remove from the pan and set aside.

Add the garlic to the pan and cook lightly.

Add wine, lemon juice, broth and artichokes and cook for about ten minutes.

Return the chicken to the pan to heat through.

Serve over rice.

MY MOM'S BRACIOLE

My Mom would make these every Sunday and put them in the sauce.

INGREDIENTS

1 pound boneless beef round, sliced into thin cutlets

1 garlic clove, finely chopped

2 tablespoons grated Romano cheese

2 tablespoons flat-leaf parsley, chopped

Salt and pepper

2 hardboiled eggs, chopped

2 tablespoons olive oil

2 garlic cloves, crushed

PREPARATION

Pound beef slices gently to about 1/4-inch thickness, or as thin as possible.

The filling:

Combine the garlic, cheese, parsley, egg, salt and pepper. Spread a teaspoon of the mixture over the beef slices. Roll up each slice and tie with a string.

In a Dutch oven, heat 2 tablespoons of olive oil. Add garlic cloves and sauté. Cook the rolls of beef, turning until the meat is browned on all sides. Place them in the sauce and simmer for two hours, turning the meat occasionally.

Josephine Traina

AUNT BEA'S VEGETABLE PIZZA

1 lb. pizza dough (see recipe next page)
Fresh spinach leaves
Sundried tomatoes, soaked in water to soften them
Red and yellow pepper strips sauteed in olive oil
Mushrooms sauteed in olive oil
Pesto sauce
Grated mozzarella cheese

Stretch pizza dough until it is thin. Brush a thin layer of pesto onto the dough. Place spinach leaves onto dough and press into place. Add sundried tomatoes, red and yellow pepper strips and mushrooms. Add mozzarella cheese and sprinkle pecorino romano cheese over vegetables.

Bake until the crust is golden brown.

AUNT BEA'S PIZZA DOUGH

1/4 ounce pkg (2 1/2 teaspoons) active dry yeast

1/2 teaspoon sugar

2 tablespoons olive oil

2 to 2 1/4 cups bleached all-purpose flour

1/2 teaspoon salt

In a large bowl, proof the yeast with the sugar in 1/3 cup lukewarm water for 10 minutes until it is foamy. Add 2 cups of flour and salt and blend the mixture until it forms a dough. Knead the dough on a floured surface for 5 to 10 minutes, until it is smooth and elastic, using as much of the remaining 1/4 cup of flour as necessary to prevent the dough from sticking.

Food Processor Method
Proof the yeast and add it to a food processor, along with 2 cups of flour and salt. Process the mixture until it forms a ball, adding more flour 1 tablespoon at a time if it's too wet. Knead the dough by processing it for 15 seconds.

Place the dough in an oiled bowl and turn it to coat it completely with the oil. Let the dough rise, covered with plastic wrap, in a warm place for 1 hour. The dough is now ready to be formed into pizzas.

Yield: Makes 1 pizza.

Josephine Traina

AUNT BEA'S ZUCCHINI PIE

INGREDIENTS

3 cups zucchini - cubed thin

1 cup onion

1 clove garlic

4 eggs

1/4 cup olive oil

1/4 cup Pecorino Romano cheese

1/2 teaspoon marjoram

1 teaspoon parsley flakes

1/2 teaspoon salt

1/8 teaspoon pepper

PREPARATION

Sauté the onion and garlic until softened. Mix all ingredients in a bowl, adding the zucchini last. Pour into a 12 inch pie plate.

Bake at 350 degrees for 30 minutes or until golden brown.

AUNT GUSSIE'S POLENTA

INGREDIENTS

4 cups water

1 teaspoon fine salt

1 cup polenta (cornmeal)

3 tablespoons butter

½ cup freshly grated Parmigiano-Reggiano cheese, plus more for garnish

PREPARATION

Step 1

For firm polenta use 4 cups water; for soft polenta use 5 cups water. Bring water to a boil in a medium-size heavy saucepan over high heat. Add 1 teaspoon of salt. Pour cornmeal slowly into water, stirring with a wire whisk or wooden spoon. Continue stirring as mixture thickens, 2 to 3 minutes.

Step 2

Turn heat to low. Cook for at least 45 minutes, stirring every 10 minutes or so. If the polenta becomes quite thick, thin it with ½ cup water, stir well and continue cooking. Add up to 1 cup more water as necessary, to keep polenta soft enough to stir. Put a spoonful on a plate, let it cool, then taste. Grains should be swollen and taste cooked, not raw. Adjust salt and add pepper if you wish.

Step 3

For firm polenta, lightly butter a baking sheet or shallow dish, approximately 8½ by 11 inches. Carefully pour polenta into the pan. Using a spatula, spread polenta to a thickness of ¾ inch. Cool to room temperature to allow polenta to solidify. Cover and refrigerate for up to 3 days. For soft polenta, add 6 tablespoons butter to the pot and stir well. Serve immediately or transfer to a double boiler set over low heat, cover and keep warm for up to an hour or so. (Or set the saucepan in a pot of barely simmering water.) Stir well before spooning into low soup bowls. Sprinkle with Parmesan, if desired.

Josephine Traina

SICILIAN STUFFED ARTICHOKES

2 lemons

3 large fresh artichokes

9 cloves garlic, sliced

4 ounces sliced Romano Cheese and/or Parmesan Reggiano Cheese sliced in 2" x 2" x 1/4" slices

1 1/4 cup Italian seasoned breadcrumbs

3 tablespoons extra virgin olive oil

Approximately 6 cups water

1. Prepare a large bowl of cool water big enough to hold the artichokes. Cut one lemon in quarters. Squeeze three quarters into the water and throw the used quarters in the bowl. Save the last lemon quarter.
2. To trim the artichoke: Remove large, hard leaves at the base. Cut the stem off to create an even base for the artichoke to sit on. With a chef's knife, lay the artichoke on its side and cut off the approx. 1-inch tip of the artichoke, including most of the leaves with sharp tips. With kitchen shears, snip any remaining sharp points off the remaining leaves.
3. With the remaining lemon quarter, rub the lemon on the cut top to prevent browning. Submerge the trimmed artichoke in the lemon water while preparing the remaining artichokes. Take out one artichoke. Turn upside down on a wooden board and press down gently with your palm to open and loosen the leaves. Turn upright, and with your fingers, firmly spread the leaves apart to make pockets.
4. Place one slice of Romano/Parmesan cheese in each leaf pocket, stuffing as many leaves as you can. The inner, light green leaves will not open.
5. Place a slice of garlic in each leaf pocket along with the cheese. Use approximately 3 cloves of garlic per artichoke.
6. Place the artichoke in a small bowl. Spread 1/2 cup breadcrumbs over the top, pushing the breadcrumbs down into the leaves with your fingers. Drizzle one tablespoon of olive oil over the top of each stuffed artichoke.
7. Place three lemon slices in the bottom of a dutch oven or large covered pot. Place the stuffed artichokes on a lemon slice. They should be stable and not tip over. Carefully pour enough water to about 1 inch in the pot, careful not to get any water on the artichokes.

8. Cover the pot and cook on medium high heat until the water boils. Lower the heat to simmer and continue steaming for about 45 - 50 minutes. Be sure to check the water level every 15 minutes and add more water if needed so it does not dry up.
9. Remove the artichokes with a large, slotted spoon to a serving plate. Drizzle with more olive oil. Serve with lemon wedges and a small bowl.

Josephine Traina

MY MOM'S STUFFED MUSHROOMS

12 large mushrooms.

1 tablespoon olive oil

1 sweet onion, chopped

2 cloves garlic, chopped

1 tablespoon chopped parsley

1/4 teaspoon salt

1/2 teaspoon pepper

1 slice bread soaked and squeezed dry

4 tablespoons breadcrumbs

Pecorino Romano cheese

Cut off stems for mushrooms and wash well. Chop stems and cook in olive oil with onion and garlic for 5 minutes. Combine mushroom stems, onion, garlic, parsley, bread, salt and pepper in a bowl until smooth. Fill each mushroom cap with the mixture. Sprinkle with breadcrumbs and cheese and drizzle with oil. Place in a greased baking dish. Bake at 400 degrees for 20 minutes.

MY MOM'S ESCAROLE (SCAROLA)

INGREDIENTS

2 tablespoons extra virgin olive oil

2 chopped garlic cloves

1 pound escarole, washed and chopped

3 cups low-salt chicken broth

Pecorino Romano cheese

salt and pepper to taste

PREPARATION

Heat 2 tablespoons of olive oil in a large pot over medium heat. Add the garlic and sauté until fragrant, about a minute. Add the escarole and sauté until wilted, about 4-5 minutes. Add a pinch of salt. Add the chicken broth and cover and simmer for about 5 minutes. Season with salt and pepper, to taste. Serve with grated cheese.

Josephine Traina

MY MOM'S POTATO CROQUETTES

4 cups leftover mashed potatoes

Pecorino Romano cheese

Unseasoned breadcrumbs

Extra virgin olive oil

Flour

3 eggs

Salt and pepper

Combine mashed potatoes, salt, pepper, grated cheese and two eggs and mix well. Form into miniature logs and roll each in flour, then in the egg wash. Roll gently in the unseasoned breadcrumbs until coated. Fry in extra virgin olive oil until light golden brown.

MY MOM'S SAUSAGE BREAD

INGREDIENTS

2 pounds hot Italian sausage removed from casing

1 tablespoon garlic, minced

1/4 cup salted butter

1 teaspoon dried parsley

2 medium sweet onions, chopped

4 cups mozzarella cheese shredded, or fresh slices

salt and pepper

2 balls of pizza dough, frozen or fresh

1 egg white

PREPARATION

1. Line a cookie sheet with non-stick foil and set aside.
2. Melt butter in a large skillet, add onions, salt, pepper, and parsley. Cook onions until they are translucent, then add the garlic. Cook the onions until they are caramelized.
3. Remove the onions to a bowl, leaving the extra butter in the pan.
4. Place the sausage in the pan and chop it into bite-sized chunks. Cook the sausage until it is browned.
5. Add the onions back to the pan with the sausage and cover with a lid. Simmer on low heat for about 15-20 minutes, stirring occasionally. DO NOT let it burn.
6. Meanwhile, preheat the oven to 350 degrees.
7. Flour the surface and roll out one dough ball with a rolling pin until it is the size of a large pizza. Avoid creating any thin spots or holes in the dough.
8. When the sausage mixture is cooked, use a slotted spoon to scoop half of it onto the dough and spread it evenly over the surface. You will save the other half for the second loaf. Cover with a layer of half the shredded mozzarella.
9. Roll up the dough like a cinnamon roll, but tuck in the ends like a burrito before you get to the end of the roll.
10. Lay it with the flap down on the cookie sheet and brush with the egg white.

11. Bake in the oven until golden brown, approximately 25-30 minutes. After baking, let the bread rest for 10 minutes before slicing.
12. Repeat process for second loaf.

MY MOM'S DOUBLE CRUST APPLE PIE

INGREDIENTS

2 3/4 cups all-purpose flour, divided, plus more for dusting

1/2 tsp kosher salt

2 sticks plus 1 tablespoon cold unsalted butter, cubed and divided

1/2 cup ice water

6 large Granny Smith apples, cored, peeled and thinly sliced

2 tablespoons fresh lemon juice

1 cup sugar

1/4 tsp cinnamon

PREPARATION

Step 1

In a food processor, pulse 2 1/2 cups of flour with the salt. Add the 2 sticks of butter and pulse until the mixture is the size of peas. Drizzle in the ice water and pulse until evenly moistened crumbs form. Turn out onto a surface and form into a ball. Divide the dough in half. Flatten into two disks and wrap in plastic, and refrigerate until firm.

Step 2

Preheat the oven to 375 degrees. Set a baking sheet on the bottom rack. In a bowl, toss the apples, lemon juice, sugar, the remaining 1/4 cup of flour and cinnamon.

Step 3

On a floured surface, use a rolling pin to roll a disk of the dough into a 13 inch round; fit into a deep 10 inch glass pie plate and brush the overhang with water. Spoon in the apples and top with the remaining 1 tablespoon of cubed butter. Roll out the second disk of dough to a 12 inch round and center it over the filling. Press the edges of dough together and trim the overhang to a scant 1 inch; fold the overlay under itself and crimp. Cut a few slits in the crust for steam to escape.

Step 4

Bake the pie in the center of the oven for 1 hour and 10 minutes, until the crust is golden. Cover the edges of the pie with foil if they begin to darken. Let the pie cool for at least 4 hours before serving.

AUNT BEA'S FRESH BLUEBERRY CAKE

INGREDIENTS

3/4 cup sugar

1/4 cup butter (soft)

1 egg

1/2 cup milk

1 teaspoon vanilla

2 cups flour

2 teaspoons baking powder

1/2 teaspoon salt

2 cups fresh blueberries

TOPPING

1/2 cup sugar

1/3 teaspoon flour

1/2 teaspoon cinnamon

Dash nutmeg

PREPARATION

Butter and flour a 9-inch x 9-inch pan. Blend together the sugar, butter and egg, mixing well. Stir in the milk and vanilla. Add flour, baking powder and salt and mix again. Fold in the blueberries. Spread the batter into the pan.

In a separate bowl, combine sugar, flour, cinnamon, and nutmeg. Stir with a fork until crumbly. Sprinkle topping over batter.

Bake at 350 degrees for 50-55 minutes.

Josephine Traina

MY MOM'S LEMON MERINGUE PIE

She used to make this especially for my father.

INGREDIENTS

PIE CRUST:

1 1/4 cups all-purpose flour 156g

1 teaspoon sugar

1/2 teaspoon salt

1/2 cup cold butter cut into cubes

3-4 tablespoons cold water

FILLING:

1 1/2 cups sugar 300g

1/2 cup corn starch 60g

1 1/2 cups water

4 egg yolks

1/4 cup lemon juice

zest from 2 lemons

2 tablespoons butter

MERINGUE:

1/2 cup water

1 tablespoon cornstarch 8g

4 egg whites

1 teaspoon vanilla

pinch of salt

1/2 cup sugar 100g

PREPARATION

PIE CRUST:

In a medium bowl, stir together the flour, sugar and salt. Cut in butter with a pastry cutter or fork until you see pea-sized chunks of butter remaining. Gradually add cold water, stirring each time until you can press it together. Form it into a disk, wrap in plastic wrap and refrigerate for at least 2 hours, or freeze for 30 minutes until chilled.

Preheat the oven to 425 degrees.
Roll out the dough to fit a 9" pie plate. Press into the pie plate and over the sides. Trim the edges and crimp or leave as desired. Poke the bottom and the sides with a fork all over to help prevent puffing (or use pie weights if you have them). Bake for 10-12 minutes until light golden brown. Set aside while you make the filling.

FILLING:

In a medium saucepan, whisk together the sugar, water, corn starch, egg yolks, lemon juice and lemon zest. Cook over medium - medium-high heat, whisking constantly, until thickened -- it will be thick, slightly thicker than pudding when warm. This can take 10-15 minutes, but don't rush it. Remove from heat and stir in butter. Pour hot filling into the pie crust and make the meringue.

MERINGUE:
Preheat the oven to 375 degrees.
In a small saucepan, whisk together the water and cornstarch. Cook over medium heat until thickened and clear. Set aside but keep warm. In a clean bowl with clean beaters, beat egg whites, vanilla and salt until soft peaks form. Gradually add in the sugar, beating until stiff glossy peaks form. Gradually add in the warm corn starch mixture, beating constantly, until completely incorporated and meringue is light and fluffy and holds stiff peaks. Spread meringue on hot pie filling (it's important that the filling is still hot!) and spread right to the edge of the pie crust. The meringue must touch the edges all the way around.

Bake at 375 degrees just until the tops of the meringue are light golden brown -- don't overbake.
Let rest on the counter on a wire rack for 1-2 hours, then refrigerate for 5-6 hours until chilled, or overnight. Slice and serve.

Josephine Traina

MY MOM'S ALMOND CRESCENT COOKIES

INGREDIENTS

1 cup butter

3/4 cup sugar

1 pinch salt

3/4 cup finely chopped fresh almonds, walnuts or pecans

2 1/2 cups all-purpose flour

If you use unsalted butter, add 1/4 teaspoon salt

1 cup confectioner's sugar

PREPARATION

Preheat the oven to 350 degrees.

In a large bowl, beat butter until fluffy. Add sugar and beat again until fluffy. Scrape down the sides of the bowl and add nuts and flour (2 cups to start, then 1 tablespoon at a time (up to 8 tablespoons if needed) and salt. Bring dough together with your fingers. Break off small pieces and form into a crescent shape. Place on ungreased cookie sheets and bake approximately 15 minutes. While cookies are still warm, roll in powdered sugar.

MY MOM'S WALNUT TARTS

INGREDIENTS

Dough

16 ounces cream cheese, softened

1 pound butter, softened

3 egg yolks

4 cups sifted flour

Filling

8 oz walnuts

2 cups light brown sugar

3 egg whites

PREPARATION

Make the dough:

In the bowl of a stand mixer, fitted with the paddle attachment, add the butter, cream cheese, and egg yolks. Cream together for 1 minute until well combined. Lower the speed and add the flour to the bowl. Mix on low speed until combined, about 2 minutes. At first the dough will look crumbly, but then it will come together. Refrigerate mixture until it is firm and not sticky to the touch.

Make the filling:

Beat egg whites until fluffy. Add brown sugar and finely chopped walnuts.

Use small muffin tins. Roll the dough into small balls and pat it into each muffin cup. Make sure the dough comes up the entire side of each cup. Place a small amount (try a teaspoon) of filling into each cup. (Don't overfill or it will bubble up and make a mess when baking).

Bake at 350 degrees for 18-20 minutes. Depending on the size of the tarts they may take a little longer to bake. They should be a nice light brown color. Remove the tarts from the mini muffin tin as soon as they come out of the oven. This will prevent tarts from sticking to the pan. Cool on wire racks.

Sprinkle tarts with powdered sugar before serving.

Makes about 36 tarts.

Josephine Traina

MY MOM'S ROSETTES

These were one of my Mom's favorites.

INGREDIENTS

2 large eggs

2 teaspoons sugar

1 cup whole milk

3 teaspoons vanilla extract

1 cup all-purpose flour

1/4 teaspoon salt

Oil for deep-fat frying

ICING:

2 cups confectioners' sugar

1 teaspoon vanilla extract

1 to 3 tablespoons water

PREPARATION

1. In a small bowl, beat eggs and sugar; stir in milk and vanilla. Combine flour and salt; gradually add to batter until smooth.
2. Heat 2-1/2 in. of oil to 375° in a deep-fat fryer or electric skillet. Place rosette iron in hot oil, then dip in batter, three-fourths up the sides of iron (do not let the batter run over top of iron). Immediately place in hot oil; loosen the rosette with a fork and remove iron.
3. Fry rosettes, a few at a time, until golden brown, 1-2 minutes on each side. Remove to paper towel-lined wire racks. Repeat with remaining batter.
4. For icing, combine the confectioners' sugar, vanilla and enough water to achieve a dipping consistency. Dip edges of rosettes into icing; let dry on wire racks.

MY MOM'S SFINGI

Sfingi are also called zeppole. (Italian doughnuts)
Eat them warm.

INGREDIENTS

1 pound ricotta cheese

4 eggs

4 tablespoons white sugar

2 tablespoons baking powder

2 cups all-purpose flour

2 quarts vegetable oil for frying

Drizzle

¼ cup honey

¼ cup confectioners› sugar for dusting

PREPARATION

1. In a large bowl, combine ricotta, eggs, sugar, and vanilla. Mix together baking powder and 1/2 cup flour. Fold into ricotta mixture. Add enough remaining flour to make a thick batter. Let rest for 1 hour.
2. Heat oil in a large heavy saucepan over high heat until a small amount of batter dropped in oil sizzles and starts to color. Drop batter by teaspoons into hot oil and deep-fry until golden. Remove with a slotted spoon and drain on paper towels.
3. Stack sfingi on a serving platter in a pyramid. Drizzle stack with honey and dust with confectioner's sugar.

Josephine Traina

MY MOM'S CANNOLI

INGREDIENTS

Shells

1 1/3 cups flour

1 tablespoon shortening

Pinch of salt

1/2 teaspoon sugar

Wine (sweet or dry)

Cannoli tubes

Vegetable oil for frying

Filling

1 pound ricotta

3/4 cup powdered sugar

1 teaspoon vanilla

Candied orange peel

Dark chocolate, grated

MAKE THE SHELLS:

Mix flour, shortening, salt and sugar. Add enough wine to make a stiff but workable dough.
Roll into a ball and let it stand for 1 hour. Roll out dough to a 1/8th inch thickness. Cut into 5" squares. Place a cannoli tube across the corners of the square. First fold one corner around the tube, then the other and press together.

Heat oil in a deep frying pan. Fry in deep fat one at a time until dark golden brown.
Remove cannoli shell carefully and let it cool before filling.

MAKE THE FILLING:

Combine the ricotta, powdered sugar and vanilla. Add the candied orange peel and grated chocolate. Fill each shell with the mixture.

AUNT BEA'S OLD FASHIONED CREAMY RICE PUDDING

INGREDIENTS

1 quart milk

1/4 teaspoon salt

1/2 cup long grained rice (rinsed and drained)

1 cup raisins

1 can evaporated milk (13 oz Carnation)

2 eggs slightly beaten

1/2 cup sugar

1 tsp vanilla

Cinnamon

PREPARATION

In a heavy saucepan, cook the milk and salt until slightly heated. Stir in the rice.

When the mixture boils, lower the heat and simmer for 15 minutes, stirring occasionally. Add raisins and cook until the rice is done, about 5 minutes. Add 1/4 cup evaporated milk and cook a few minutes longer. In a mixing bowl, combine the eggs, sugar, vanilla and the remaining 3/4 cup evaporated milk. Stir some of the rice mixture into the egg mixture. Return this mixture to the saucepan and cook slowly until it thickens a bit, about 3 minutes. Pour it into a bowl and stir pudding while it cools. Serve with a sprinkle of cinnamon.

Josephine Traina

MY MOM'S NEW YORK CHEESECAKE

Servings: 8 to 10

Prep Time: 30 Minutes

Cook Time: 1 Hour 55 Minutes

Total Time: 2 Hours 25 Minutes, plus at least 8 hours to cool

INGREDIENTS

FOR THE CRUST

1 1/2 cups graham cracker crumbs, from 12 whole crackers

5 tablespoons unsalted butter, melted

2 tablespoons sugar

1/8 teaspoon salt

FOR THE FILLING

32 oz (four 8-oz blocks) cream cheese, at room temperature

2 cups sugar

3 tablespoons all-purpose flour

4 teaspoons vanilla extract

1 teaspoon packed lemon zest, from 1 lemon

2 teaspoons fresh lemon juice, from 1 lemon

1/4 teaspoon salt

6 large eggs

1/2 cup sour cream

Special equipment: 9 or 10-inch springform pan; 18-inch heavy-duty aluminum foil

PREPARATION

INSTRUCTIONS FOR THE CRUST

Preheat the oven to 375°F and set an oven rack in the lower middle position. Wrap a 9 or 10-inch springform pan with one large piece of heavy-duty aluminum foil, covering the underside and extending all the way to the top so there are no seams on the bottom or sides of the pan. Repeat with another sheet of foil for insurance. Spray the inside of the pan with nonstick cooking spray.

Make the crust:

In a medium bowl, combine the graham cracker crumbs, melted butter, sugar, and salt. Stir until well combined. Press the crumbs into an even layer on the bottom of the prepared pan. Bake the crust for 10 minutes, until set. Remove the pan from the oven and set aside.
Reduce the oven temperature to 325°F. Set a kettle of water to boil.

Make the batter:

In the bowl of an electric mixer fitted with the paddle attachment or beaters, beat the cream cheese, sugar, and flour together on medium speed until just smooth, about 1 minute. Scrape the bottom and sides of the bowl to be sure the mixture is evenly combined. Add the vanilla, lemon zest, lemon juice, and salt. Beat on low speed until just combined. Add the eggs, one at a time, mixing on low speed until incorporated, scraping the bowl as necessary. Mix in the sour cream. Make sure the batter is uniform but do not over-mix.

Check to make sure your oven has cooled to 325°F, then set the cheesecake pan in a large roasting pan. Pour the batter on top of the crust. Pour the boiling water into the large roasting pan to come about 1 inch up the side of the cake pan.
Bake until the cake is just set, 1 hour and 30 minutes to 1 hour and 45 minutes. (If the cheesecake starts to look too golden on top towards the end, cover it loosely with foil.) The cake should not look liquidy at all but will wobble just a bit when the pan is nudged; it will continue to cook as it cools.

Carefully remove the roasting pan from the oven and set it on a wire rack. Cool the cheesecake in the water bath until the water is just warm, about 45 minutes. Remove the springform pan from the water bath and discard the foil. If necessary, run a thin-bladed knife around the edge of the cake to make sure it's not sticking to the sides (which can cause cracks as it cools), then cover with plastic wrap and transfer to the refrigerator to cool for at least 8 hours or overnight.

For serving:

Remove the sides of the springform pan. Serve the cheesecake right from the base of the pan; or, to transfer it to a serving platter, run a long, thin spatula between the crust and the pan bottom, and then use two large spatulas to carefully transfer the cheesecake to a serving dish. Slice with a sharp knife, wiping the knife clean between slices. Serve with berry sauce, or Lucky Leaf Cherry Filling.

Josephine Traina

MY MOM'S SOUR CREAM COFFEE CAKE

INGREDIENTS

1/2 cup butter softened

3/4 cup sugar

1 teaspoon vanilla

3 eggs

1 pint sour cream

3 cups flour

3 teaspoon baking powder

1 teaspoon baking soda

1/2 teaspoon salt

Filling:

1/2 cup chopped walnuts

1/2 cup sugar

2 teaspoons cinnamon

2 or 3 teaspoons unsweetened cocoa powder

PREPARATION

In a large mixer bowl with a paddle attachment, beat together the butter, sugar, vanilla, eggs, and sour cream until they form a smooth batter. Sift together the flour, baking powder, baking soda and salt. Add flour mixture to the batter. Beat until well combined. Make the filling. Combine the walnuts, sugar, cinnamon and cocoa. Pour half of the batter into a greased and floured tube baking pan or Bundt pan. Sprinkle half of the filling over the batter. Add the rest of the batter. Sprinkle with the rest of the filling. Bake at 350 degrees for 45 minutes. Cool on a wire rack. Remove the cake from the pan.

MY MOM'S PIGNOLATA

Fried balls of dough dipped in honey and topped with sprinkles. Made in Italy during the Carnevale and also a favorite around Christmas. My Mom and I would stay up until 2 o'clock in the morning making these.

INGREDIENTS

3 cups all-purpose flour

3 tablespoons granulated sugar

1/4 teaspoon salt

4 large eggs

3 tablespoons vegetable oil

1 tablespoon milk

vegetable oil (canola or sunflower oil may be used) for frying

1 cup honey

colored candy sprinkles for serving

PREPARATION

Prepare the dough:

Combine flour, sugar and salt either in a bowl or in a mound directly on your counter. Make a well in the center and add the eggs, vegetable oil and milk. Use a fork to beat the eggs and slowly incorporate the flour into the wet ingredients until a raggedy dough is formed. Transfer to your counter and knead until a smooth dough is formed. Cover and let rest at room temperature for 30 minutes. Divide the dough into 4 pieces. Roll into long ropes (as you would for making gnocchi) about 1/2 inch thick. Cut into 1/2-inch pieces. Leave the pieces as is or if you prefer, roll each into a ball. Transfer the pieces onto a baking sheet, not overlapping, to prevent them from sticking together.

Fry the pieces in the hot oil until golden brown. Remove with a slotted spoon. Drain on paper towels.

Heat the honey in a saucepan. Add the pignolata in batches to coat them with the honey. Stack the pignolata in paper cupcake liners, forming a mound in each one. Add a few sprinkles to each.

Blossoming With Grace at Every Age

Left: Mama Nonne, undated | Right: Author today

When I was a little girl, I was confused about why all my grandparents looked so old, and I vowed that when I grew up, I would not age like them. I come from a long line of little Italian women with hunchbacks (the burdens they carried), as well as a tendency for osteoporosis. I, too, noticed my body was aging similarly to Mama Nonne's. I found her immigration record, which showed her as five feet tall and weighing 138 pounds. I am 5 feet, 1 inch tall and weigh 122 pounds. I am not aging like my great-grandmother or my mother.

I've learned I don't have to age like my ancestors. You can change the way you age by being aware of the family patterns you are running, of illness, or a lack of physical strength. You can reverse the aging process and regenerate yourself to a younger version. The Mediterranean diet, exercise, a curious desire to learn and grow and stretch yourself all contribute. They help the transformation that will start to regenerate you as your cells get replaced by healthier, younger versions. It's already happened for me, and it can happen for you.

You can blossom differently. You don't have to be riddled with medicines and illnesses. It's a choice you can make today. As I enter the last quarter of my life, I want to make every day count and be as vital a human as possible and to reach the ultimate goal of being the very best version of myself. I have removed the word aging from my vocabulary. I choose to say I am blossoming with grace. You can choose the same.

Bibliography

BOOKS

Cornelisen, Ann. *Women of the Shadows*. Boston/Toronto: An Atlantic Monthly Press Book, Little, Brown and Company, 1976.

Edelman, Hope. *Motherless Daughters: The Legacy of Loss*. Cambridge, MA, Da Capo Press, 2006.

Jackson, Kenneth T., Manbeck, John B., Citizens Committee for New York City. *The Neighborhoods of Brooklyn*. Citizens for NYC, Yale University Press, [New York], New Haven, 2004.

ONLINE RESOURCES

"A City of Villages," Library of Congress Classroom Materials. Accessed January 23, 2023. https://www.loc.gov/classroom-materials/immigration/italian/a-city-of-villages/

Ancestry.com - https://www.ancestry.com/

"Bushwick, Brooklyn," Wikipedia, last edited 23 February 2023. https://en.wikipedia.org/wiki/Bushwick,_Brooklyn

Chronological List of Brooklyn Parishes, 1822-2008 https://dioceseofbrooklyn.org/wp-content/uploads/2012/10/chronological_list_brooklyn_parish_school_2012.pdf

"Doctor," National Park Service, last updated December 13, 2016. https://www.nps.gov/elis/learn/historyculture/people_doctor.htm

"Ellis Island," Library of Congress Classroom Materials. Accessed January 23, 2023. https://www.loc.gov/classroom-materials/immigration/italian/ellis-island/

"Ellis Island," History.com, last updated February 13, 2023, History.com Editors. https://www.history.com/topics/immigration/ellis-island, A&E Television Networks

Familysearch.org - https://www.familysearch.org/en/

Genealogy.com - https://www.genealogy.com/

Gjenvick-Gjonvik Archives, last updated 2023 - https://www.ggarchives.com/index.html

"The Great Arrival," Library of Congress Classroom Materials. Accessed January 23, 2023. https://www.loc.gov/classroom-materials/immigration/italian/the-great-arrival/

"Immigration and Relocation in U.S. History: Italian," Library of Congress Classroom Materials. Accessed January 23, 2023. https://www.loc.gov/classroom-materials/immigration/italian/

"Italian Immigration to Providence," STEAMing Into The Future. Accessed January 23, 2023. https://shiphistory.org/2017/07/10/immigration-to-providence/

"Leaving Europe: A New Life in America" Exhibition, Digital Public Library of America (DPLA), Europeana. Texts, research and compilation by Joan Krizack and Sieger Verhart. Accessed January 23, 2023. https://www.europeana.eu/en/exhibitions/leaving-europe

Marx, Karl, "Sicily and the Sicilians," *New-York Daily Tribune*, No. 5948, May 17, 1860. Marx and Engels Collected Works, Volume 17 (pp.370-372), Progress Publishers, Moscow 1980. http://marxengels.public-archive.net/en/ME1199en.html

National Archive. "INS Boards of Special Inquiry (BSI) Records," last reviewed June 7, 2022. https://www.archives.gov/research/immigration/boards-of-special-inquiry#:~:text=Specifically%2C%20the%20act%20required%20that,one%20of%20the%20excluded%20classes.

"New York, New York, Index to Passengers Lists of Vessels, 1897-1902", database, *FamilySearch* (https://www.familysearch.org/ark:/61903/1:1:ZG9T-1TT2 : 30 July 2020), Baldassare Rizzuto, 1900.

"New York Passenger Arrival Lists (Ellis Island), 1892-1924", database with images, *FamilySearch* (https://familysearch.org/ark:/61903/1:1:JXZT-WZ8 : 2 March 2021), Petronilla Augileri, 1900.

"SHIPS - Italian Immigration to U.S. in the Early 20th Century," YouTube. Accessed January 23, 2022. https://youtu.be/p_mIi6if2fs

"Sicilian Genealogy," Times of Sicily. Accessed January 23, 2023. https://www.timesofsicily.com/category/lifestyle/sicilian-genealogy/

"Sicilian Naming Convention," Coniglio Family Website, last revised March 19, 2022. http://coniglio-family.com/ http://www.conigliofamily.com/SicilianNamingConvention.htm

The Statue of Liberty–Ellis Island Foundation, Inc, last updated 2023. https://www.statueofliberty.org/ellis-island/

"Tenements and Toil," Library of Congress Classroom Materials. Accessed January 23, 2023. https://www.loc.gov/classroom-materials/immigration/italian/tenements-and-toil/

The 1911 Triangle Factory Fire, Cornell University, ILR School, Kheel Center, 2018. https://trianglefire.ilr.cornell.edu/victimsWitnesses/victimsList.html

Tsigalou C, Konstantinidis T, Paraschaki A, Stavropoulou E, Voidarou C, Bezirtzoglou E. Mediterranean Diet as a Tool to Combat Inflammation and Chronic Diseases. An Overview. Biomedicines. 2020 Jul 8;8(7):201. doi: 10.3390/biomedicines8070201. PMID: 32650619; PMCID: PMC7400632. https://www.ncbi.nlm.nih.gov/pmc/articles/PMC7400632/

"Under Attack," Library of Congress Classroom Materials. Accessed January 23, 2023. https://www.loc.gov/classroom-materials/immigration/italian/under-attack/

"Vita, Sicily", Wikipedia, last edited 17 January 2022, https://en.wikipedia.org/wiki/Vita,_Sicily

"Vita, Sicily." Accessed February 27, 2023. http://www.sicily.co.uk/nearby_town/vita/

"What is Epigenetics?" Centers for Disease Control and Prevention, last updated August 15, 2022. https://www.cdc.gov/genomics/disease/epigenetics.htm

CENSUS RECORDS

Angerline Angerlara [Angela Angeleri], Year: *1900*; Census Place: *Brooklyn Ward 16, Kings, New York*; Roll: *1053*; Page: *20*; Enumeration District: *0247*; FHL microfilm: *1241053*

Baldosras Lagrasoa [Baldorras Lagrassa], Year: *1900*; Census Place: *Brooklyn Ward 16, Kings, New York*; Roll: *1053*; Page: *20*; Enumeration District: *0247*; FHL microfilm: *1241053*

Peter La Franse, Year: *1910*; Census Place: *Brooklyn Ward 27, Kings, New York*; Roll: *T624_980*; Page: *13B*; Enumeration District: *0841*; FHL microfilm: *1374993*

Peter Lagrassa [Peter La Grassa] Year: 1900; Census Place: Brooklyn Ward 16, Kings, New York; Roll: 1053; Page: 20; Enumeration District: 0247; FHL microfilm: 1241053

Peter Lagrosa, New York State Archives; Albany, New York; State Population Census Schedules, 1905; Election District: A.D. 15 E.D. 15; City: Brooklyn; County: Kings; Page: 73

Peter Lagrassa, New York State Archives; Albany, New York; *State Population Census Schedules, 1915*; Election District: *15*; Assembly District: *19*; City: *New York*; County: *Kings*; Page: *89*

Baldasare Rizzulo, Year: *1910*; Census Place: *Brooklyn Ward 27, Kings, New York*; Roll: *T624_980*; Page: *13B*; Enumeration District: *0841*; FHL microfilm: *1374993*

Baldassore Rizzuto, 1920 census, *Brooklyn Assembly District 19, Kings, New York*; Roll: *T625_1175*; Page: *56B*; Enumeration District: *1208*, Ancestry.com (February 2023)

Henry Rizzuto, New York State Archives; Albany, New York; *State Population Census Schedules, 1915*; Election District: *15*; Assembly District: *19*; City: *New York*; County: *Kings*; Page: *89*

Pietronilla Rizzuto, Year: *1920*; Census Place: *Brooklyn Assembly District 19, Kings, New York*; Roll: *T625_1175*; Page: *56B*; Enumeration District: *1208*

Peter Rizzuto, New York State Archives; Albany, New York; *State Population Census Schedules*, *1915*; Election District: *15*; Assembly District: *19*; City: *New York*; County: *Kings*; Page: *89*

Josephine Sciacca, New York State Archives; Albany, New York; *State Population Census Schedules*, *1925*; Election District: *02*; Assembly District: *19*; City: *Brooklyn*; County: *Kings*; Page: *1*

Nick Sciacca, *Census, 1925* [database on-line]. Provo, UT, USA: Ancestry.com Operations, Inc., 2012. Original data:State population census schedules, 1925. Albany, New York: New York State Archives. *State Population Census Schedules, 1925*; Election District: *02*; Assembly District: *19*; City: *Brooklyn*; County: *Kings*; Page: *2*.

Neck Skiacca, Year: *1940*; Census Place: *New York, Kings, New York*; Roll: *m-t0627-02607*; Page: *7A*; Enumeration District: *24-2321*

BIRTH, MARRIAGE & DEATH RECORDS

Angela Angeleri, New York City Department of Records & Information Services; New York City, New York; *New York City Death Certificates*; Borough: *Brooklyn*; Year: *1908*

John Dolzani, New York City Municipal Archives; New York, New York; Borough: *Brooklyn*. Ancestry.com. *New York, New York, U.S., Marriage License Indexes, 1907-2018* [database on-line]. Lehi, UT, USA: Ancestry.com Operations, Inc., 2017.

Marie Formica, New York City Department of Records & Information Services; New York City, New York; *New York City Death Certificates; Borough: Brooklyn; Year: 1932*

Find a Grave, database and images (https://www.findagrave.com/memorial/159103033/marie-formica: accessed 11 March 2023), memorial page for Marie Formica (unknown–Oct 1932), Find a Grave Memorial ID 159103033, citing Saint John Cemetery and Mausoleum, Middle Village, Queens County, New York, USA; Maintained by cfenters (contributor 46996728).

Marie Formica [Marie Angeleri], New York City Department of Records & Information Services; New York City, New York; *New York City Death Certificates*; Borough: *Brooklyn*; Year: *1932*

Salvatore Impellizzeri, New York City Municipal Archives; New York, New York; Borough: *Brooklyn*. Ancestry.com. *New York, New York, U.S., Marriage License Indexes, 1907-2018* [database on-line]. Lehi, UT, USA: Ancestry.com Operations, Inc., 2017.

Find a Grave, database and images (https://www.findagrave.com/memorial/208475603/salvatore-impellizzeri: accessed 04 April 2023), memorial page for Salvatore Impellizzeri (29 Aug 1918–16 Sep 2016), Find a Grave Memorial ID 208475603, citing Saint Anthonys Church Cemetery, Nanuet, Rockland County, New York, USA; Maintained by Michael McCue (contributor 47317791).

Giuseppina La Grassa, New York City Department of Records & Information Services; New York City, New York; *New York City Death Certificates*; Borough: *Brooklyn*; Year: *1928*

Find a Grave, database and images (https://www.findagrave.com/memorial/164941708/josephine-guiseppina-la_grassa: accessed 11 March 2023), memorial page for Josephine Guiseppina *Angeleri* La Grassa (5 Aug 1859–19 Oct 1928), Find a Grave Memorial ID 164941708, citing Saint John Cemetery and Mausoleum, Middle Village, Queens County, New York, USA; Maintained by Lostnwyomn (contributor 47168791).

Baldassre Rizzuto, New York City Department of Records & Information Services; New York City, New York; *New York City Death Certificates*; Borough: *Brooklyn*; Year: *1927*

(https://www.findagrave.com/memorial/169206089/baldassare-rizzuto: accessed 28 February 2023), memorial page for Baldassare Rizzuto (unknown–4 Jul 1927), Find a Grave Memorial ID 169206089, citing Saint John Cemetery and Mausoleum, Middle Village, Queens County, New York, USA; Maintained by Grddgtr2grvdggr (contributor 48679319).

Giuseppa Rizzuto, *New York City Births, 1891-1902*; Title: *Births Reported in 1900. Borough of Brooklyn.*; Certificate #: *17835.*

Josephine Rizzuto, New York City Municipal Archives; New York, New York; Borough: *Brooklyn. Ancestry.com. New York, New York, U.S., Marriage License Indexes, 1907-2018 [database on-line]. Lehi, UT, USA: Ancestry.com Operations, Inc., 2017.*

Pietro Rhizzuto, *New York City Department of Records & Information Services; New York City, New York; New York City Death Certificates; Borough: Brooklyn; Year: 1904*

Pietro Rizzoto, Ancestry.com. *New York, New York, U.S., Birth Index, 1910-1965* [database on-line]. Lehi, UT, USA: Ancestry.com Operations, Inc., 2017. Original data:New York City Department of Health, courtesy of www.vitalsearch-worldwide.com. Digital Images.

Pietronell Rizzuto, Social Security Administration; Washington D.C., USA; *Social Security Death Index, Master File.*

Find a Grave, database and images (https://www.findagrave.com/memorial/170098482/pietronella-rizzuto: accessed 08 March 2023), memorial page for Pietronella Rizzuto (unknown–Jan 1968), Find a Grave Memorial ID 170098482, citing Saint John Cemetery and Mausoleum, Middle Village, Queens County, New York, USA; Maintained by Grddgtr2grvdggr (contributor 48679319).

Maria Anna Sciacca, Ancestry.com. *New York, New York, U.S., Birth Index, 1910-1965* [database on-line]. Lehi, UT, USA: Ancestry.com Operations, Inc., 2017.
Anna M. Sciacca, New York City Municipal Archives; New York, New York; Borough: *Brooklyn. Ancestry.com. New York, New York, U.S., Marriage License Indexes, 1907-2018 [database on-line]. Lehi, UT, USA: Ancestry.com Operations, Inc., 2017.*

Josephine Traina

Crocifissa Sciacca, New York City Municipal Archives; New York, New York; Borough: *Brooklyn*. Ancestry.com. *New York, New York, U.S., Marriage License Indexes, 1907-2018* [database on-line]. Lehi, UT, USA: Ancestry.com Operations, Inc., 2017.

Josephine Sciacca, New York City Department of Records & Information Services; New York City, New York; *New York City Death Certificates*; Borough: *Brooklyn*; Year: *1934*

Josephine Sci Acta, *Brooklyn Times Union; Publication Date: 11 Jun 1934; Publication Place: Brooklyn, New York, USA; URL: https://www.newspapers.com/image/576223884/?article=28b0c890-2229-4b10-97d9-7d5b590d-6b57&focus=0.51426417,0.9295569,0.63897413,0.97695917&xid=3355*

Find a Grave, database and images (https://www.findagrave.com/memorial/169738754/josephine-sciacca: accessed 08 March 2023), memorial page for Josephine Sciacca (unknown–12 Jun 1934), Find a Grave Memorial ID 169738754, citing Saint John Cemetery and Mausoleum, Middle Village, Queens County, New York, USA; Maintained by Lostnwyomn (contributor 47168791).

Nicola Sciacca, New York City Municipal Archives; New York, New York; Borough: *Brooklyn*. Ancestry.com. *New York, New York, U.S., Marriage License Indexes, 1907-2018* [database on-line]. Lehi, UT, USA: Ancestry.com Operations, Inc., 2017.

Nicolo Sciacca, Ancestry.com. *New York, U.S., New York County Supreme Court Naturalization Petition Index, 1907-1924* [database on-line]. Provo, UT, USA: Ancestry.com Operations Inc, 2000.

Sciacca, Nicolo, Ancestry.com. *U.S., Find a Grave™ Index, 1600s-Current* [database on-line]. Lehi, UT, USA: Ancestry.com Operations, Inc., 2012. Original data: *Find a Grave™*. Find a Grave. http://www.findagrave.com/cgi-bin/fg.cgi.

Pietrina Sciacca, Ancestry.com. New York, New York, U.S., Birth Index, 1910-1965 [database on-line]. Lehi, UT, USA: Ancestry.com Operations, Inc., 2017.

Petronilla P. Sciacca, New York City Municipal Archives; New York, New York; Borough: *Brooklyn*. Ancestry.com. *New York, New York, U.S., Marriage License Indexes, 1907-2018* [database on-line]. Lehi, UT, USA: Ancestry.com Operations, Inc., 2017.

Find a Grave, database and images (https://www.findagrave.com/memorial/195069429/anna-m-traina: accessed 20 March 2023), memorial page for Anna M. Traina (27 Apr 1922–21 Jun 1991), Find a Grave Memorial ID 195069429, citing Fairfax Memorial Park, Fairfax County, Virginia, USA; Maintained by JimL (contributor 48920443).

Charles J. Traina, New York City Municipal Archives; New York, New York; Borough: *Brooklyn*. Ancestry.com. *New York, New York, U.S., Marriage License Indexes, 1907-2018 [database on-line]. Lehi, UT, USA: Ancestry.com Operations, Inc., 2017.*

History & Family Discoveries

BUSHWICK, BROOKLYN

Bushwick, Brooklyn was one of Kings County's original six towns. Its name was derived from the Dutch Boswijck, meaning 'neighborhood in the woods.' Located between Broadway and Flushing Avenue, it was primarily a farming community which produced food and tobacco for local consumption and for export to New York. Bushwick boomed from 1840-1860 when many German-speaking immigrants came to the United States. Adrian Mortense Suydam started to subdivide his family farm in 1869. By 1884, there were at least 125 multi-family homes constructed throughout the neighborhood. By 1890, there were fourteen breweries within fourteen blocks. The ethnic composition of Bushwick changed after the Great Depression, as the percentage of German Americans declined during the 1930s and 1940s, and the neighborhood became home to a greater proportion of Italian and Sicilian immigrants. The Broadway and Myrtle Avenue rail line reached the area and eased the commute to Manhattan.

SWEATSHOPS

Women and men working in garment factories were exposed to infectious diseases and the risk of fire. The International Ladies' Garment Workers' Union (ILGWU) organized a strike for better wages and safer working conditions in 1909, known as "Uprising of the 20,000." Women strikers won a 52-hour work week and a 12-15% wage increase, but workers' safety demands and recognition of the union as the workers' representatives were rejected. Safety was not a priority for sweatshop owners. By 1910, most garment workers were young immigrant girls and seventy percent of them were Sicilians and Italians or Russian Jews. Most were illiterate or had no work qualifications.

On Saturday, March 25, 1911, a fire which started in a scrap bin at the Triangle Shirtwaist Factory in lower Manhattan, killed 146 and injured 78 of the 500 people working that day. Most of the victims were Sicilian and Italian and Jewish immigrant women and teenage girls who did not speak English. They worked twelve hours a day in a crowded environment full of sewing machines and fabric. The danger of fire in garment factories was well known, but often no useful precautions were taken to ensure the safety of the immigrant workers. The victims died from smoke inhalation and other injuries, because of locked stairwells and exit doors. The fire is remembered as one of the most infamous incidents in American

Josephine Traina

industrial history since the deaths were largely preventable. Michael Hirsh, an amateur genealogist, and historian, spent years researching the names of the victims of the fire, combing through newspapers, census records and other vital records and eventually compiling a complete list, which can be found at Remembering The 1911 Triangle Factory Fire.

From the 1900s to the 1930s, labor strikes, labor and community organizing, and investigations of factories eventually led to legislation and heightened public awareness about acceptable labor standards. These activities laid the groundwork for federal New Deal reforms in the 1930s, designed to eliminate sweatshops and strengthen unions.

The men and women in my family worked in sweatshops, where they were undoubtedly subjected to unsafe working conditions and infectious diseases. Mama Nonne, her husband, Baldassare, her sisters, Angela, Maria, and Josephine, her niece, Christina, her daughter Josephine, and her granddaughters, Beatrice and Gussie, were among the brave souls who worked and sacrificed to support their families. Mama Nonne lied about her age and worked in factories well into her seventies. May their sacrifices never be forgotten.

Peter LaGrassa & Josephine Angeleri LaGrassa

Mama Nonne's sister, Josephine, and her husband, Peter LaGrassa, had three children in Sicily, Salvatore, Christina, and Baldassare (Benjamin). Peter was the first family member to travel to America in 1898, and his efforts made it possible for my family to have a start in America. Their descendants would be our remaining link to Mama Nonne's original family. Baldassare also had four siblings about whom we know very little.

Peter and Josephine moved around Brooklyn a lot, but they lived at 124 George Street, the building Mama Nonne and Baldassare would eventually own, for several years. Their entire family became naturalized citizens. Their children married and had children of their own. Salvatore followed in his father's footsteps and worked as a piano maker for a time. Christina was widowed young and worked in factories to support her family. Benjamin was the first in the family to attend college, and he eventually became a teacher at Forth Hamilton High School in Brooklyn.

Josephine Traina

LAGRASSA FAMILY TREE

↓

Peter LaGrassa & Josephine Angeleri *married in Sicily*
- Salvatore *(1890-1939)*
- Christina *(189?-1967)*
- Baldassare (Benjamin) *(189?-1980)*
  - Josephine *(1859-1928)*
  - Peter *(1862-1949)*

↓

Salvatore & Josephine Rizzuto
married 1909
- Josephine *d. 1910*
- Salvatore & Teresa Ruisi
  married 1911
- Salvatore *d. 1939*
- Teresa *d. 1977*

Christina & Louis Profera
married 1909
- Rosina *b. 1910*
- Joseph
- Josephine
- Louis
- Louis *d. 1921*
- Christina *d. 1967*

Benjamin & Catherine McCue
married 1930
- Arthur
- Jordan
- Benjamin *d. 1980*
- Catherine *d. 2002*

↓

Rosina & Jerome Parlato
- Frank
- Louis
- Jeanette
- Jerome *d. 1983*
- Rosina *d. 1992*

Joseph & Jean Profera
- Joan
  divorced 1972
- Joseph *d. 1988*

Josephine & Domenick Alu
- Richard
- Josephine *d. 2004*

Louis & Antoinette Profera
- Kathleen *b. 1943*
- Michael *b. 1947*
- Louis *d. 1983*
- Antoinette *d. 2011*

Recipes Index

My Italian Wedding Soup	57	My Mom's Stuffed Mushrooms	82
My Mom's Pasta Fagioli	59	My Mom's Escarole (Scarola)	83
Aunt Bea's Vegetable Soup	60	My Mom's Potato Croquettes	84
My Mom's Andy Boy Broccoli	61	My Mom's Sausage Bread	85
My Marinara Sauce	62	My Mom's Double Crust Apple Pie	87
Aunt Gussie's Saint Joseph's Day Recipe - Pasta Milanese	63	Aunt Bea's Fresh Blueberry Cake	89
My Mom's Pesto	64	My Mom's Lemon Meringue Pie	90
My Chicken Parmigiana	65	My Mom's Almond Crescent Cookies	92
My Stuffed Shells With Cheese Or Meat	66	My Mom's Walnut Tarts	93
My Bison Bolognese	68	My Mom's Rosettes	94
My Oven Baked Bison Meatballs	70	My Mom's Sfingi	95
My Mom's Spiedini (Italian Kebabs)	71	My Mom's Cannoli	96
My Mom's Eggplant Parmesan	72	Aunt Bea's Old Fashioned Creamy Rice Pudding	97
Aunt Bea's Chicken With Artichokes	74	My Mom's New York Cheesecake	98
My Mom's Braciole	75	My Mom's Sour Cream Coffee Cake	100
Aunt Bea's Vegetable Pizza	76	My Mom's Pignolata	101
Aunt Bea's Pizza Dough	77		
Aunt Bea's Zucchini Pie	78		
Aunt Gussie's Polenta	79		
Sicilian Stuffed Artichokes	80		